THE

INTERNATIONAL SERIES

IN THE BEHAVIORAL SCIENCES

EDITED BY

John E. Horrocks

THE OHIO STATE UNIVERSITY

Houghton Mifflin books in Psychology
are under the general editorship of
LEONARD CARMICHAEL

Muzafer Sherif

In Common

Social Psychology of Intergroup

Predicament

Conflict and Cooperation

Houghton Mifflin Company · Boston

New York · Atlanta · Geneva, Ill. · Dallas · Palo Alto

ACKNOWLEDGMENTS

Material quoted from *Aggression: A Social Psychological Analysis,* by L. Berkowitz, pages 8, 23, 24, and 141, used by permission of McGraw-Hill Book Company. Copyright © the McGraw-Hill Book Company.

Quotations from C. E. Osgood, *An Alternative to War or Surrender,* pages 138–139, are used by permission of the University of Illinois Press.

Quotations from T. H. Pear, *Psychological Factors of Peace and War,* pages 40–41 and 64, are used by permission of the Philosophical Library.

Quotations from R. Emerson, *From Empire to Nation,* pages 197–198, 359, 414, and 402, are used by permission of the Harvard University Press.

Material quoted from J. P. Scott, *Aggression,* pages 33, 34, 35, 62, and 99, is used by permission of The University of Chicago Press. © by The University of Chicago. Published 1958.

Material from *Old Myths and New Realities and Other Commentaries,* by J. William Fulbright, pages 73–74 and 86–87, is reprinted by permission of Random House, Inc. and Jonathon Cape Ltd. © Copyright 1964 by J. William Fulbright.

TO

GARDNER MURPHY

Editor's Foreword

Man is a paradox: solitary and gregarious, friendly and hostile, cooperative and disruptive. He can build and he can destroy. As a social being, he must work with others for his own and for the common good. But as a biological entity bent upon survival, his is the law of the jungle. The social aspect becomes a façade behind which his egocentric needs run their course. Yet in a world inhabited by so many, the cooperative-social man must hold his egocentric-biological side in check if civilization as we know it is to survive. Man's great task remains that of somehow resolving the social and biological conflict so that he may live in harmonious concert with his fellows, simultaneously serving his own needs and those of the common enterprise.

That this task is a formidable one the long history of man's inhumanity to man, of war, and of personal conflict bear witness. Yet there is the equally long history of human kindness, selflessness, and common endeavor. If man has demonstrated his warlike and selfish nature, he has also shown his hunger for peaceful co-existence and cooperation. In today's world of increasing population, tremendous technological efficiency, and scientific advances that make a mockery of time and space and threaten us with annihilation, man must rise above himself if he is to endure. He must conquer his paradox. He must live in amity with his fellows and work with them to bring about a world in which there will be a tomorrow and in which he can play the role of the civilized, social being rather than of the predatory animal.

But how is he to accomplish this? What understandings does he need? What action must he take? How successful can he hope to be? It is to these essential questions that Professor

Sherif addresses himself in *In Common Predicament*. He has presented an empirically based, conceptually integrated psychology of intergroup relations. He has advanced hypotheses about conditions likely to promote hostile attitudes and intergroup conflicts, and has taken the further step of explaining how such attitudes and conflicts, once aroused, may be reduced. But he does not rest his case here. He has also proposed a program of research for further testing of his hypotheses.

As Professor Sherif views it, the origins of intergroup hostility cannot be traced to a few disaffected persons. Such hostility is created by all those who compose a given group of whatever size and nature. The hostile relationships are seen to arise from certain interactions between groups. To the degree that there is solidarity *within* a group, its approach to *outside* groups becomes more rigid — either for better or for worse. Essentially, the reduction of hostility between groups is achieved by focusing the attention of each group on external, common goals that can best be attained by cooperative action. Even as social norms regulate relationships between individuals, so do they regulate relationships between groups, providing a key to the understanding of intergroup transactions at any level. Social norms that support group self-concepts of superiority or nurture group awareness of inferiority lead only to intergroup hostility. In contrast, social norms that support the dignity of man, the right of peoples to self-determination and equality of opportunity lead to the reduction of intergroup hostility and conflict. When the goals are shared, an area of "we–ness" embraces distinct groups which, in their shared and agreed upon destiny, become one; and group members justify or condemn events related to the area of "we-ness" in terms of their assessment of the impact of the event upon the common enterprise. Experience of a common predicament is a tie that binds conflicting groups more firmly than any other commonality. Common opposition is also a unifying force. But unfortunately cooperation tends to fade when the common predicament or opposition ceases to exist.

The argument is developed and analyzed, and solutions are

advanced. Will the solutions work, and what are the probabilities of success? The background of the Sherif's original research — viz., the induction of conflict and its subsequent amelioration in groups of twelve-year-old boys — does not at first seem to hold promise of extension to the larger stage of adult affairs and the arena of international relations. Yet the child sets the prototype for the adult, and human nature is constant whether revealed in little boys, or adults, or in the interrelationships of whole nations and races. The microcosm of the individual is reflected in the macrocosm of the many, for the many are only one multiplied many times.

The group has no existence apart from the individuals who compose it, and the psychology of the group must be approached through the common human psychology of its members. The group is the artifact, and its individual members with their human motives and behavior are the group's composers and creators. Increase in the size of the group adds only problems of logistics and communication. It adds nothing else of basic importance. Yet, having emphasized this truth, we must go on to observe that man is shaped and influenced by his context, and as a member of a group he does not act alone. He is as much influenced by the group consensus as by his own perception. We may even say that the group consensus *becomes* the individual's perception, and he is no longer free to test reality. But, though these appear paradoxical elements, the individual still acts as an individual in the light of what the group consensus has taught him. His individual psychology is operative even as he responds to the influence of his group, but he is chained by the point of view and the reinforcements of his culture.

This is a timely book for an era when group is pitted against group, when misunderstanding is rife, and when the speed of communication makes for immediate confrontation of groups whose contacts were once insulated by distance and time. The modern world has become a world of change, analysis, self-searching, disintegration, and fear. Old ways, old positions of status and power, and old objectives must be examined and re-examined. Yet our contemporary problems are still rooted in the interpersonal relationships of the people who make up our world, and so it is particularly appropriate to examine the dynamics of those interrelations. Professor Sherif has provided such an examination.

JOHN E. HORROCKS

The Ohio State University
Columbus, Ohio

Preface

For close to twenty years, a substantial part of the research program in social psychology that Mrs. Sherif and I have carried out has been devoted to the vital problem area of intergroup relations. It is an area that embraces all the major topics of social psychology and, for that matter, of psychology in general — perception, learning, emotion, motivation (aggression, cooperation, frustration), categorizing, stereotyping, effects of group membership. These topics cover a vast territory, and yet the study of intergroup relations demands more than the orthodox scope of the trained psychologist. An adequate social psychology of intergroup relations requires heavy borrowing from the social sciences (anthropology, political science, sociology), for the states of friendship and enmity that characterize the problem of intergroup relations are also the concern of these disciplines. Whenever the psychologist formulates hypotheses without close attention to the relevant findings of the social sciences, the questions he raises and the generalizations he arrives at can have only tangential bearing on the actualities of intergroup relations. The issue at stake is that of the *validity* of research findings.

During the last twenty years, our work proceeded with keen awareness of the crucial issue of validity. The awareness is reflected in our various research projects and publications, which include *Groups in Harmony and Tension* (1953) and *Intergroup Conflict and Cooperation: The Robbers Cave Experiment* (1954, 1961), as well as our chapters in *Intergroup Relations and Leadership* (1962), in *Perspectives in Social Psychology* (1965, Klineberg and Christie, eds.), and in *Behavioral Science and Human Survival* (1965, Milton Schwebel, ed.).

The need for a viable social psychology of international relations has clearly become the most urgent of human needs under the impact of technological revolution in both the military and industrial spheres, conflicting social systems, the disintegration of colonialism, and the rise of new nations all over the world from the debris of two wars of global proportions. *In Common Predicament* represents an effort to supply such a social psychology. It is based on and is an extension of our previous works. We have made an attempt to synthesize and to extend the implications, particularly in Chapters 6–9, where the analysis moves steadily towards the international level. The mode of analysis and the unmistakable intergroup trends described in the last chapter have implications for a world body (*a* united nations) that is truly *binding* on all constituents. However, it proved to be too huge a task to document and spell out all the implications in this small volume. This must wait for a future publication.

I am grateful for the tangible help and cooperation that I received from various people. My appreciation goes to the members of my various seminars on intergroup relations. In the more recent ones, I want to single out Donald Granberg, George Appley, Joan Rollins, and Samuel Shurtleff. Others have been acknowledged in our previous writings.

For typing and retyping the first drafts of these chapters, I am grateful again to Mrs. Betty Frensley of Norman, Oklahoma. The final, revised manuscript was typed with patience and skill by Mrs. Doris Sands of State College, Pennsylvania.

The surveys on various nationalisms prepared for me in the late 1950's by Dr. Bertram Koslin, now of Princeton University, and Dr. Nicholas Pollis, now of Oklahoma State University, while they were associated with our program have been useful. The ever-ready and understanding cooperation of Dr. John Horrocks, editor of the International Series in the Behavioral Sciences, is appreciated.

I am grateful to Dr. Lewis Wade Jones, Fiske University, and to Dr. Maurice H. Merrill, Research Professor of Law, the University of Oklahoma, for the unpublished material they provided for use in this book. These contributions are utilized, in condensed form, in Chapters 6 and 9 respectively.

My appreciation is extended to President George L. Cross and his administrative associates, Dr. Kyle McCarter and Dr. Lloyd Swearingen, of the University of Oklahoma, for creating the conditions necessary for concentration on research and writing. I owe similar appreciation to the administration of the Pennsylvania State University for making it possible for me to concentrate on the revision of this book while serving in a visiting capacity in 1965–66.

Carolyn W. Sherif shared with me all the effort of putting together the material to go into this book, in organizing it through long hours of discussion, in writing much of what are probably its best chapters, and, not least, in going through the prolonged efforts and pain of revision. In spite of this she has resisted my urging that she share the title page with me. Yet, I want to make it clear that this is a Sherif and Sherif work like several others published earlier.

For some years, we have been waiting for an opportunity to express our gratitude to our friend Gardner Murphy, who believed in our efforts to conceptualize a realistic scientific social psychology. It was Gardner Murphy who urged me thirty years ago to write *The Psychology of Social Norms* when I presented to him an outline of my projected norm-formation experiments utilizing the autokinetic effect and their underlying theoretical rationale. It was in a discussion with him about three years ago that I decided to write a book like this. And it is gratifying to dedicate it now to Gardner Murphy because it deals with a problem that has consistently been of utmost concern to him — how to encourage a selfless and persistent devotion to peace and decency among human beings.

MUZAFER SHERIF

University Park, Pennsylvania
May 2, 1966

Contents

Contents

1

Problem

This book presents the psychology of the most overriding, the most anxiety-ridden, and therefore the most challenging of human problems in the modern world. The problem is subsumed under the label "intergroup relations," a label increasingly in the limelight on the contemporary scene. The label "intergroup relations" has come to refer to the states of friendship or enmity, cooperation or competition, conflict or harmony, alignment or nonalignment between groups and combinations of groups, small or large.

Intergroup relations include the vexing problems of minority peoples in various nations who are struggling to achieve equal rights, against prevailing arrangements based on supremacy premises. They encompass labor-management friction, and the search for more lasting solutions to prevent their recurrence. They encompass alignments and nonalignments between political parties, factions, and ideological camps. Towering above all intergroup problems are those raised by the alignments, nonalignments, and counteralignments among various nations: both the old established nations and the newly emerging nations who are restless, yet determined to claim their place in the sun on an equal footing with former mentors or rulers.

Intergroup attitudes revealing like or dislike, love or hate, trust or distrust, good will or malicious intent, claims of supremacy or equality are powerful emotional instigators of people's designs and deeds in their dealings with others. But these strong emotions, powerful passions, intense attitudes, and their associated images are not self-generated springs to action. They do not erupt spontaneously from *human nature in the raw* to instigate their design and action toward others. These instigators of feeling and action are generated psychologically when people transact with other people, in the course of carrying out activities and pursuing goals within the design of living they have patterned.

Any unit of people, small or large, poor or rich, downtrodden or mighty, has some unique sense of self-identity or of common predicament. But this sense of identity as a unit of people is not a primitive intuition that unfolds spontaneously. The sense of self-identity emerges with all its unique characteristics and shadings when people are shaping the unit itself.

There is no predetermined or immutable blueprint for the formation of a given number of persons into a new human unit. People form and re-form human groupings when they feel the necessity of participating together in toil toward common objectives, or as they share success or failure, glory or humiliation. During the process of formation, the experiences shared by people result in a sense of identity differentiating themselves as a unit. For example, people who are downtrodden, subjugated, or oppressed, barely surviving in dire poverty, begin to forge a sense of identity when they formulate their common rejection of the oppressor and join in opposition to him.

The formation of a human grouping wider than the bounds of family and immediate locality enlarges the psychological relatedness of persons composing it so that a wider physical territory is appropriated as *theirs*. The scope for the new psychological bounds of the identity depends on the size, technological means, political orientation, and common interests of the unit in question. Thus, while expanding the experience of human relatedness, the formation of enlarged human groupings once again circumscribes the sense of identity of their members within new bounds, at times making it highly exclusive.

Every human grouping generates goals that are revealed through the strivings of its identified members. The scope and character of these goals, as well as the zeal and efficiency with which they are pursued, are affected by the organizational structure of the grouping, its political orientation, its human, material, and technological resources. In pursuing their goals, human groupings and their subunits necessarily come into relationship with other units with goals and designs of their own.

Goal objects and facilities, coveted real estate and resources, people courted as allies, people discarded and detested by a group do not exist in a special universe reserved for the designs of one particular grouping. They are within the range of the designs of other human groupings. The real or imagined compatibility or incompatibility between one group's attainment of goal objects and the designs of other people arouses moves to pull together with those other people or to pull away from them, to help or hinder them. As these moves proceed, they are accompanied by feelings of cooperativeness or jealousy, mutual support or resentment, liking or disliking, compromise or unyielding opposition.

Speaking generally, the mere awareness of other groups within the range of our designs generates a process of comparison between "us" and the others. This tendency seems to be one of the fundamental facts in the psychology of judgment. In this comparison process, we evaluate and categorize other groupings of people, comparing them with our notions of ourselves, our conceptions of our place in life and the places of others. The basis for the evaluation is a scheme for defining the scope and character of humanity that has been built into our particular groupings and practiced as we pursue cherished goals. The attitudes and images of any human grouping toward other peoples are codifications justifying our actions toward others. This proposition is clarified and documented in Chapter 2.

The Problem and the World Today

It follows from our discussion of the feelings, emotions, and attitudes toward other people that the psychology of intergroup attitude and action necessarily becomes *social* psychology. Specification of the enormous task at hand as a task of social psychology simply underscores our starting point: intergroup attitudes with their emotions that instigate our actions toward other groupings are not self-generated psychologically. They are generated in the course of interchanges among people who have formed a sense of identity, as they pursue their goals in a world peopled by others who also have their own aspirations and make their own moves to attain them. This conclusion has implications for theories of human aggression, as we shall see in Chapter 3.

The psychological events (intergroup attitudes) as well as the decisions and lines of actions in various nations today are related to the living context of which they are parts. If this context is omitted, the psychology of intergroup relations is doomed to the fate of being inconsequential. It can only yield incoherent bits of contradictory information. The living context of intergroup attitudes and actions consists of the interlocking ties among ever-enlarging human groupings, many of them new. It represents an irreversible state of dependence between peoples across continents.

With modern facilities, nations and blocs are now within easy reach of one another, within easier reach than Philadelphia or Paris for people who lived within the radius of a few hundred miles from these cities at the times of the American and French Revolutions. They are also very much within the scope of each other's concerns. They are mutually mindful of happenings everywhere. They are highly sensitized to evaluate events for their bearing on themselves. Nations and blocs of nations regard it as imperative to look over one another's shoulders constantly. They feel duty-bound to be up to date on the political stability, industrial development, resources, accomplishments, and weaknesses of other nations and blocs. They are concerned about the strengthening or weakening of their ties and commitments to others.

Even the mightiest and wealthiest nations have become interested in knowing their image in the eyes of others. They want to have a favorable image, even in the eyes of peoples in far corners of the world, people with different skin colors, people with customs that seem to them strange and "wild" who live in locations they once considered out of their world with names only a few consider worth pronouncing correctly. They go far out of their way in efforts to improve their image.

Such concerns are symptoms of a state of dependence among groupings that cuts across traditional cultures, religions, political bodies, and ways of life. It effective scope is no narrower than the world itself. Apart from this state of dependence how can anyone in his right mind make sense of contemporary events? A once mighty empire, which dazzled others in its splendid exclusiveness in social relations, sends dignitaries from the apex of its social hierarchy to represent it at the independence celebrations of new nations that were once possessions, like India, Ghana, or Kenya. Full power is transferred to leaders who only a few years earlier were thrown in jail by the same empire as disorderly and incorrigible enemies of peace and order. Full honor is accorded to those who were once represented as villains responsible for destruction of life, orderly progress, and civilized conduct.

Should we, in search of an explanation, resort to the versatile vocabulary of psychological jargon? Could such events indicate a tendency toward self-inflicting masochism? Is there a tendency inherent in the depths of human nature to "identify with the aggressor"? We can only say that if human nature has such inherent tendencies, they must be of recent origin. In earlier periods, the formation of new nations did not enjoy the representation of such a galaxy of dignitaries from former rulers. The United States of America, for example, was not so honored by King George.

In the heyday of a great colonial power, the tearing of its flag, the loss of life by a few of its citizens, the damage of their property or other interests were followed, as a rule, by show of force. Naval might, land forces, or marines appeared. A great power once did not hesitate to take the law into its own hands, even over rather minor disputes, with little or no regard for the feelings and reactions of the rest of the world.

Today, facing deeds of greater proportions, the decision-making process toward possible courses of action is guided with somewhat more restraint and with more deliberate anticipation of consequences. There is concern over the impact on neighbor and stranger, friend and foe in the rest of the world. Today, a nation that takes the law into its own hands to subdue another by force is subject to denunciations by peoples around the globe. No matter how great its power, it must expect a swelling chorus of protests to join the lonely voice of its victims.

Today, policy-makers can ill afford to consider decisions solely in terms of the slight or damage inflicted upon some of their citizens. Their policy is not dictated entirely by the designs of their own people or by interest groups clamoring for action. At the same time, policy-makers must be mindful of how others, outside their national boundaries, will evaluate the lines of action in question. How "the rest of the world" will evaluate and label a course of action has to be taken into account, no matter how strongly the policy-makers themselves may feel that the course of action is justified.

Psychologists who theorize on the role of frustration in producing aggressive intent and action can ill afford not to broaden their perspective through the analysis made by political scientists on the use of force in the context of the present state of affairs. For example, Rupert Emerson (1960) concluded after a comprehensive survey of relations between older and emerging nations: "The use of force, once so easily engaged in, had now become more damaging than helpful and had lost its stamp of legitimacy. The evidence indicated that anti-colonialists could take to arms to better effect and with greater impunity than could the once mighty Europeans" (p. 402).

The neat framework of the usual psychological research truncates the context of aggressive action by chopping off the past and the future consequences. It would require a tortuous string of psychological terms from that framework to tackle the intergroup attitudes, decisions, and lines of action that characterize the traffic between nations today. The existence, the viability, and the development of every nation today are regarded by the rest of the world as more than just "internal affairs" of that particular nation. These matters have become an urgent concern for all, no matter how remotely the nation is situated, no matter how "underdeveloped" it is, no matter how different its way of life may appear in Western eyes, according to orthodox Western premises.

The great powers are diverting huge sums of money, earthly goods, facilities, and skilled manpower into various aid programs to many nations all over the globe, despite unfinished business at home urgently calling for solutions, despite pockets of poverty at home and unfinished plans to streamline home industry in phase with the tempo of the nuclear age. At times the great powers compete to be the foremost in such aid programs. They even congratulate themselves when their aid program is accepted by a new nation, especially one they consider strategic.

This state of affairs may be examined fruitfully from the point of view of another psychological mode of analysis: the effects of rewards and punishments in controlling behavior. The response in the nation receiving aid from another country is by no means always gratitude and alignment with the donor. Cases of alignment with rivals of the donor are not rare. As cogently concluded by Rupert Emerson (1960) from rich illustrative material, "the outlook for gratitude among nations is not encouraging. States are likely to accept aid where they find it, without too scrupulous examination of the source, as witness India, Egypt, and Guinea among others" (p. 414).

Doubtless, the disappointment of the donor when a recipient reveals ingratitude on a series of trials is a punishing experience. But the donor's response is not always an unmeditated reversal of policy, contrary to the prediction of psychological theories of reinforcement formulated within the narrow context of the orthodox psychological research.

Neither recipient nations nor donors regulate their attitudes and actions solely in terms of immediate rewards, reversals, or rebuffs. The recipient nations no doubt find the aid rewarding, as well as the expressions of cordial acceptance and the public declarations of equality accorded them, especially by their former rulers. But they view the aid as the means for standing on their own feet and for developing themselves in the family of nations. Rightly or wrongly, they often view the aid as overdue partial payment for plunder they endured over long decades in the past. They may consider the declarations of equality, cordiality, and zealous attention to their dignity as acts of atonement for the humiliation and exploitation they suffered at the hands of their former rulers, who justified their acts on premises of superiority.

Many new nations see their present and future predicament tied to that of other nations who have also emerged from degrading humiliations of the past. Thus, the effective framework within which the orientations, attitudes, decisions, and actions of new nations are forged is not defined solely by the reward or withdrawal of aid. The effective framework includes forms such as Pan-Africa, Pan-Asia, or Pan-Africa-Asia movements and councils. Nations tend to chart their courses, their alignments, nonalignments, and orientations to the future within such frameworks, not exclusively in terms of their problems within their present boundaries. With the past still fresh in their memory, they are highly sensitive to the grim consequences of divide-and-rule policies so effectively utilized in the past.

Unless such guideposts to the framework shaping the attitudes and decisions by new nations are examined, there is little possibility of explaining their behavior. This is the context in which many new nations appear sensitive, suspicious, and ready to hurl labels of "schemer," "aggressor," and "imperialist" at the designs and actions of former colonial rulers and their allies, even when a particular plan may have been advanced with the purest of intentions from thoroughly humanitarian motives.

The illustrative examples of contemporary intergroup attitudes and actions are not presented to pass a value judgment on any nation. There is no intention of assessing "who is to blame" in any such case. In the present state of increasing dependence of nation upon nation and continent upon continent, there are research tasks much more pressing than assessing "who is to blame" in a particular dispute. Probably it is more important to assess what typically happens when determination of blame is attempted.

Casting blame by peoples actively confronting each other in disputes is usually futile for arriving at a solution. It ordinarily intensifies the stand of each party, strengthening their negative views of each other and thus sustaining animosities. Assessment of blame for contemporary intergroup conflicts embroils both researcher and participants in a vicious circle spiralling back into time. It is an ideal medium for revealing the particular selectivity and partiality of the researcher through his choice and interpretation of facts, as we shall see in Chapter 7.

The illustrative cases of intergroup attitude and behavior today were given to emphasize the need for a theoretical framework that provides a proper context to account for them. Without this context, many attitudes and behaviors exhibited by peoples in conflict or alliance seem contradictory. It is not surprising that some accounts of intergroup events attribute them to spiteful freaks of a "human nature" that has been improvised in post mortem analysis.

The Needed Perspective

Psychology has been terribly myopic in its approach to the study of human relations. The typical research design has been constructed largely in terms of tradition or of the researcher's convenience. In our craze to reduce the variables to those that are conveniently at our fingertips, the factors that actually set boundaries for human relations have been mutilated. Usually, the variables are confined arbitrarily to those the researcher can manipulate easily in selected interpersonal relations. Even the physical setting and social context of these selected interpersonal encounters have often been neglected.

No set of interpersonal relations is a closed system today. The passions, goals, and designs that prevail within the restricted web of interpersonal ties are not self-generated events. Their roots spread into the setting in which the interpersonal encounters take place.

Many statements have been made on the importance of a proper framework for studying attitude, sentiment, and behavior of individuals. Psychology is full of truisms on the topic, but very little has been done in actual research practice to incorporate the variables in such a framework. The orthodox complacency is hard to overcome.

A proper framework for the study of intergroup attitudes and behavior is imperative today. We cannot do justice to events by extrapolating uncritically from man's feelings, attitudes, and behavior when he is in a state of isolation to his behavior when acting as a member of a group. Being a member of a group and behaving as a member of a group have psychological consequences. There are consequences even when the other members are not immediately present. The orthodox custom of taking these consequences for granted amounts to ignoring them. It has resulted in serious miscalculations of behavioral outcomes, as many experiments have demonstrated during the last thirty years.

Similarly, there is a misleading fallacy in the uncritical extrapolation from findings about relations of people *within* groups to make predictions on *inter*group relations. In the modern world, no grouping or nation is an island unto itself, no matter how powerful or how weak, no matter how developed or underdeveloped its technology. The increasing dependence of one upon another has consequences *within* groups and nations, and *between* groups and nations.

Within nations, the trend is towards strengthening the nation-wide identifications of subunits, with values and cherished goals that imply widening of outlooks, attitudes, and loyalties of members. The trend is toward resolution in favor of a national identity, when the national value orientation is at odds with that of local, tribal, or regional custom and vested interest.

Between nations, the trend is towards formations enlarged beyond the exclusiveness of the national boundary and sovereignty. This trend is revealed in movements such as Pan-African and Pan-Asian movements and in regional, continental, and intercontinental meetings. It is revealed in bloc alignments and counteralignments, in political moves toward an Organization of African States, Organization of American States, and the like. The trend is revealed in moves toward giant alliances of the major ideological camps, which tower above geographical distinctions.

Finally, the trend towards larger human formations and the enlarged identification and loyalty they ultimately require is reflected in the conception, if not in the actuality, of the United Nations — conceived in the blood, tribulations, and dislocations of two major world wars. In spite of the imperfections of its organization, in spite of divisive bloc and ideological power politics, the United Nations has at times exerted a moral influence that was unthinkable in previous periods.

The interlocking state of dependence among nations has been brought about through man's accomplishments in science and technology, production, transportation, and communication. It cuts across continents, affects ideological camps, and touches the plans

of everyone. Henceforth, no nation may be insulated, including
the most mighty and wealthy. No nation's fortune is now its own
exclusive business. Each constitutes a link in an interlocking chain,
wherein the collapse of one has unmistakable reverberations
throughout the entire system. Above this irreversible state of
dependence of one upon all, and all upon one, hangs the ominous
shadow of a nuclear war. Descent of this shadow would leave no
refuge for the cultural heritage of centuries, nor for life itself.

The theme of this work is the social psychology of attitudes and
behavior of people who live in an ever-enlarging system. Within
this interlocking system of groupings, each has become the other's
keepers, not only in a moral sense but in the sense that each
becomes the other's killer if either fails to choose a creative alternative to a deadly showdown.

In order to pursue this theme, let us start by indicating the scope
of intergroup relations studies in human affairs today.

CURRENT TOPICS OF INVESTIGATION

The study of intergroup relations has come irrevocably to the
foreground as a result of actualities in human affairs today: the
sharp razor edge between war or peace in a tense world; the dependence of nation upon nation for the existence and development
of each; the unfinished business left by human arrangements and
doctrine based on the premises of supremacy entertained by
privileged and dominant peoples.

Many research projects have been undertaken by universities, by
governments, by United Nations agencies, by specially instituted
enterprises, and by mushrooming action agencies with diverse
programs. There is little coherence or coordination in these efforts.
They shoot in all directions. The political scientist, the sociologist,
the economist, and the psychologist, as well as the policy-maker,
office-holder, and the military are involved in these activities, each
in his own way.

The following list, far from complete, gives an idea of the variety
and scope of contemporary research activities in the area of intergroup relations:

Studies on attitudes, stereotypes, and social distance, and
various methods of changing them (for example, through exchange of students and professors, person-to-person contacts,
conference methods, communication).

Studies related to psychological theorizing conducted both by psychologists and nonpsychologists on human impulses toward aggression, dominance, cooperation, and submission; on possible consequences of frustration; on "displaced" aggression; and on the impact of certain child-rearing practices on intergroup hostility and the development of aggressive attitudes.

Studies of social, legal, political, and economic aspects of discrimination, with particular reference to issues raised by segregation practices in various countries.

Studies of intergroup relations in industry, especially with reference to labor-management problems. Some of these studies are subsumed under the "human relations" approach in the United States.

Studies of political party rivalries, party tactics, pressure groups, and "extremist" movements.

Studies related to problems of emerging nationalism vis à vis a declining colonialism.

Studies of "factionalism" in cultures undergoing acculturation at an accelerated pace under the impact of modern technology and military arrangements.

Studies of diplomacy, strategy, war, and peace, using such methods as content analysis and "rational" models of decision-making.

An extensive survey and evaluation of any or all of the above lines of research will not be undertaken here. Our task is the statement of a coherent social psychology of intergroup relations based on representative literature on the topic and a systematic research program during the last fifteen years. A great deal of the background is reported in our *Groups in Harmony and Tension* (1953). The details of research design, procedures, and analysis of results are presented in previous works (Sherif, 1954; Sherif and Sherif, 1956; Sherif *et al.*, 1961).

DEMARCATION OF THE PROBLEM

Before we can develop an adequate framework for studying intergroup behavior, the problem must be defined. This is not an idle matter. Many technically excellent studies have fallen short in dealing with intergroup attitude, policy, and action because they were not designed on the basis of an adequate characterization of intergroup relations.

Not every friendly or unfriendly act toward others is a case of intergroup behavior. Not all policy-making or decision is an intergroup action. We have to differentiate those actions that can be properly called intergroup behavior.

Let us start by specifying the main concepts involved. Necessarily, we must begin with an adequate conception of the key term, "group." We define a group as a social unit that consists of a number of individuals (1) who, at a given time, have role and status relationships with one another, stabilized in some degree and (2) who possess a set of values or norms regulating the attitude and behavior of individual members, at least in the matters of consequence to them. Shared attitudes, shared sentiments, shared aspirations and goals that characterize the closely identified members are related to these properties, especially to the common values or norms of the group.

Group norms are the expected, and even ideal modes of behavior, defining for members the bounds of acceptable behavior. Thus, a norm is not *necessarily* a statistical average of observed behaviors by persons in a group. The expected or ideal modes of behavior defined by norms relate to motives and goals members share in common. They concern the existence and perpetuation of the group itself. They regulate the reciprocal expectations of members in the functioning of the organizational pattern.

Intergroup relations refer to relations between two or more groups and their respective members. Whenever individuals belonging to one group interact, collectively or individually, with another group or its members *in terms of their group identification,* we have an instance of intergroup behavior.

The appropriate frame of reference for studying intergroup behavior is the functional relations between two or more groups, which may be positive or negative. The functional relationship between groups whose members perceive them as *in-groups* has properties of its own. These properties are generated during interaction *between* the groups. Intergroup situations are not voids.

Though not independent of the relationships within the groups in question, *the characteristics of functional relations between groups cannot be deduced or extrapolated solely from the properties of relations that prevail among members within the group itself.* Prevailing modes of behavior within groups (such as cooperativeness and solidarity, or competitiveness and rivalry among members) need not be the prevalent modes of behavior in their relations with other groups. Hostility toward the out-group may, at times, be proportional to the degree of solidarity within the group. Democracy at home need not imply democratic attitudes toward out-groups.

Some Blind Alleys in Conceptions of Intergroup Behavior

Frequently, intergroup relations have been explained through analysis of individuals who have suffered unusual degrees of frustration, or who have received extensive authoritarian treatment in their early life histories. There is good reason to believe that some persons growing up in unfortunate circumstances may become more intense in their prejudice and hostility towards persons outside their groups. But such cases are not the crux of the problem of intergroup relations. At best, they can explain the *intensity* of behavior in directions already discernible in their group. On the whole, established stereotypes of out-groups are not the doings of a few frantic or frustrated individuals.

When there is conflict between two groups (such as a strike or a war), the more responsible, the more talented, the more exemplary members of the groups are usually in control. Activities in conflict are conducted by individuals who can withstand the strains imposed by the conflict. When members of a group *correctly* or *incorrectly* perceive threat, unjust treatment, or invasion of their rights by another group, opinion in their group is consolidated, slogans are formulated, and decisions are made for effective measures. Those recognized as responsible take the lead. Deviate personalities or highly frustrated members ordinarily exhibit their intense reactions within the range or latitude for acceptable behavior established in their respective settings. The latitude of acceptable behavior may include hostility toward other groups as well as sacrifice for one's own.

If intergroup behavior were first and foremost a matter of understanding the behavior of exceptionally disturbed individuals, it would not be the issue of vital consequence that it is today. I repeat: *intergroup behavior is not primarily a problem of deviate behavior.* In stable times, it is primarily a problem of participation by individual members within the bounds of established norms for social distance between groups. In periods of flux and change, such as that characteristic of our own times, it is a problem of participation in trends developing between groups led by members who are regarded as responsible by their fellows.

On the basis of UNESCO studies in India, Gardner Murphy (1953) concluded in his book, *In the Minds of Men,* that to be a "good" Hindu or a "good" Moslem at the time, implied believing all the nasty qualities and practices attributed by one's own group to the adversary. The "good" members, who usually constitute the overwhelming majority, remain deaf and dumb to favorable or correct information disseminated concerning their adversary. On the whole, occasions for further conflicts arise during social contacts or when the avenues for communication between them are opened.

It has been argued that aggressive behavior directed against other groups is a result of pent-up aggressive impulses accumulated by group members owing to their individual frustrations. Otto Klineberg asked penetrating questions in this regard in his survey of *Tensions Affecting International Understanding* (1950). "Why, if war is due to these factors within the individual, are the majority of individuals opposed to war? Why must they be made to fight? Why must every country, in seeking to build its army, have recourse to conscription?" (p. 199).

Modern warfare is conflict between social units with definite organizations and value systems. It is not simply a sum total of personal frustrations among the populations translated into aggressive acts.

L. T. Richardson (1950) compiled statistics on the number of wars engaged in by major world powers from 1850 to 1941. Britain heads the list with twenty wars — more than the Japanese (with nine), the Germans (with eight), or the United States (with seven). In the years following World War II, we heard explanations of Germany's warlike tendencies on the basis of the authoritarian character of the German family and educational system with resulting frustration to the individual German. Do Richardson's statistics indicate that the British people were more frustrated than the Germans? In this connection, it seems reasonable to ask a question that historians and political scientists can help us answer: "Doesn't having an empire with far-flung interests to be protected and expanded have anything to do with the frequency of war?"

Today we are told that it would be extremely difficult for the United States to remain aloof from a major conflict in any part of the world, since it is one of the major powers. Does the democratic or authoritarian upbringing of the individual American in Iowa or Maine or Arizona have anything to do with the likelihood of the United States being involved or not being involved in a war? Are those persons most inclined toward war the most frustrated persons in the country?

Framework for Intergroup Behavior

Such considerations lead to conclusions concerning the effects of motivational components (for example, aspirations, frustrations, aggressive impulses) at different levels of interaction — individual, group, and intergroup interaction.

We cannot legitimately explain behavior in groups by extrapolating from information about each individual's motivational urges and frustrations. The interaction processes and reciprocities within a group have definite properties that affect behavior. Compelling material conditions (for example, technology and socioeconomic forces) in which a group functions influence behavior in a group, as do the existing organizational structure and the system of beliefs prevailing in the larger society. Oscar Lewis has demonstrated this in a striking way in his book, *Five Families* (1950), which has in its subtitle the phrase "the culture of poverty."

We cannot extrapolate from the properties of individuals to the characteristics of group situations. It is equally erroneous to extrapolate from the properties of relations *within* a group to explain relations *between* groups, as though the area of interaction between groups were a vacuum, or even the cozy atmosphere of a conference room (*cf.* Katz, 1960). The character of the relations and norms prevailing within groups does influence relations with other groups, but this is not the whole picture. Intergroup relations are potently determined by the process of interaction *between* the groups. The give-and-take between groups may be full of conflict or in a state of flow. This area of conflict or of cooperation may produce consequential reverberations within the groups themselves (Sherif and Sherif, 1953).

What determines the positive or negative nature of interaction between groups? In large part, it is the reciprocal interests of the groups involved and their relative significance to the group in question. The issues at stake between groups must be of considerable concern to the groups, if they are to play a part in intergroup relations. They may relate to values or goals shared by group members, a real or imagined threat to the safety of the group, an economic interest, a political advantage, a military consideration, prestige, or a number of others. Once a particular issue comes to the foreground in intergroup relations, it may become the *limiting factor* in the interaction between them, dominating their other mutual concerns.

LEADERSHIP, POLICY-MAKING, AND REPRESENTATION AS GROUP FUNCTIONS

Within groups, whether small or large, formal or informal, the focus of power resides in the leader and other high status members. But leadership itself represents a status and a function *within* a group, and not *outside* it, as Cecil Gibb (1954) concluded in his comprehensive survey of leadership studies. The leader himself is not immune from sanctions if he deviates too far from the bounds of acceptable behavior prevailing in his group.

Leaders, delegates, and representatives of the groups must remain a part of the power structure of the group if their actions are to be effective. The significance of the group's power structure for assessing the behavior of persons in such positions may be seen when their actions deviate widely from the expectations of the membership. In matters concerned with the existence, self-identity, well-being, and safety of the group, expectations for its leader are more exacting than for others in lesser positions. These exacting expectations for the man in a leadership position are proportional to the power and initiative invested in him. He cannot afford to have an image of being "soft" in his dealings with the adversary.

This is illustrated, for example, by the fate of one O'Brien, who once was leader of the elite ore-trimmers' union at a Lake Michigan port. As president of the union, he was sent to Cleveland to negotiate a pay scale for the coming season. Instead, he became involved in a deal to transfer his men to a new union — one that would trim ore for less than he was delegated to demand. When he began to carry out the scheme upon his return, the rank and file were aroused and indignant at his sell-out. When the men caught up with him, "O'Brien was ready for ten months in a hospital and nobody on the street seemed to know who had prepared him" (Holbrook, 1946).

The tragic fates of the World War I French hero Marshal Petain and of former Premier Laval, who went far beyond the bounds of loyalty to collaborate with the Nazi invaders, are among the well known cases that need no elaboration.

Delegation and representation of authority are integral aspects of group functioning, especially in relations with other groups (see Chapters 7 and 8). Studies by Ralph Stogdill and his associates show that within a large organization, subordinate members expect superiors to delegate authority and regard those who delegate more freely as better leaders. Yet Stogdill, in his book *Individual Be-*

havior and Group Achievement (1959), observes that there are limiting situations "where a high degree of co-ordination is required," and delegation may result in "confusion and mis-directed effort" (p. 189).

Thus, in critical situations, leaders tend to take over the reins. If representatives in a collective bargaining situation are not making effective headway, the top leaders may, for the first time, get *directly* into these procedures. Similarly, a critical international situation temporarily reduces the authority of representatives on international councils. At such times top leadership may step to the front line of negotiations, as illustrated in various summit meetings of recent times.

In dealings between groups, power is manifested in different ways. Within a large organization or within a society, relations between groups are ordinarily subject to sanctions by the still larger organization. However, in a "casually patterned" society, to use sociologist Robert Lynd's characterization (1945), the relations between some of the constituent organizations may not be regulated by sanctions applicable to all parties within the larger organization. These areas of intergroup relations—in what Bierstedt (1957) has called the "unorganized interstices" of society — are in the foreground of major social problems in this country today.

In relations between nations, the extent of regulation by commonly accepted sanctions is still smaller. Thus, power is not infrequently manifested in the form of force or threat of force. It is in such contexts that relationships between groups become vital to the survival of the groups in question.

THE TASK UNDERTAKEN IN THIS BOOK

It is sobering to face the task of writing a book on the vast and fateful problem area of relations between human groupings. Transactions between peoples take diverse forms in the modern world. The factors ultimately affecting their give-and-take or their clashes are varied. Ultimately, they include all aspects of human society.

There is no pretense here to take any one specific case of intergroup relations in its full detail, much less to outline the conditions which can enter decisively in major confrontations in a modern, highly technological world. The undertaking is much less, yet in another sense, it is much more.

The purpose of this book is to outline an orientation to the *social psychology* of intergroup relations that embodies the essential features and thus can encompass the various factors that may enter into any specific case. It aims at an outline that will be valid when applied to any particular case of intergroup relations and its specifics.

Since the major gaps in knowledge on intergroup problems concern the conditions for effective reduction of intergroup tension and conflict, the book develops toward this focus. It would be feasible, of course, to apply the orientation toward more detailed analysis of various kinds of intergroup conflicts and their course.

Chapter 2 discusses the role of the past in shaping intergroup attitude and action. Specifically, it concentrates on those cases in which the past becomes a heavy hand in dealing with current intergroup problems. Therefore, both the origins of group images and the psychological processes whereby men acquire categorizations to evaluate themselves and others are considered.

Chapter 3 examines major traditional doctrines about the psychological springs of human aggression, evaluating the doctrines in the light of recent research findings and new developments based on them. The major doctrine discussed is psychoanalytic theory, with its varied modern versions in "psychodynamic" formulations.

With these empirical and critical foundations, Chapter 4 outlines guideposts for the research orientation that accommodates the essential features of intergroup problems. A research program designed and executed on this basis is summarized in Chapter 5.

The question of the validity of the orientation is seriously considered in the remainder of the book. Chapter 6 presents experimental verifications and extensions of the research, as well as applications in the areas of industrial relations and civil rights struggles.

In Chapter 7, certain traditional practices in dealing with intergroup problems are analyzed within the perspective gained from the research. The practice of casting blame for intergroup conflict by parties in controversy is scrutinized. The research results throw a particularly revealing light on the fundamental errors in solutions proposing deterrent strategies or "balance of power." Despite the fact that such strategies are political-military, their fundamental error is found in their assumptions about human psychology.

Chapter 8 considers in some detail the conditions necessary for various measures to become effective in reducing conflict between groups, especially information campaigns, conferences among leaders and representatives, and person-to-person contacts. In line with the indications of the research program, evaluation of these measures points to the *necessity of a motive base* for such measures to be effective in reducing intergroup hostility, singly or in combination. The motive base is provided by superordinate goals, which are goals urgently felt by all parties in conflict that can be attained only through concerted efforts on the part of all parties involved.

The implications of conclusions reached about the rise and reduction of intergroup conflict are applied in the final chapters to intergroup relations on the larger scene in the contemporary world, with particular attention to the growing dependency of group on group.

2

When the Past Becomes
a Heavy Hand

When people meet, their behavior is affected by the transactions between them. Give-and-take among strangers, friends, or enemies colors each of us, at least while it lasts. Such interactions can be traced in social psychological analysis. However, the immediate interchange of words, or gestures and activities does not weave the whole fabric of personal encounters.

Any instance of immediate interaction among persons contains threads from the past and projected webs of the future. "Can we be friends?" "Can I do business with him?" "I can trust these people." "This is a person to be respected." "He is out to ruin me for good!" In such terms we reflect our efforts to base our actions toward others on past experiences and to behave appropriately, according to our own aims for the future.

The intermeshing of past, present, and image of the future in human relationships is not confined to encounters between members of different groups. But for several reasons, the comprehension of here-and-present actions in many intergroup encounters requires considerable knowledge of past events and future designs. Consider the following documented examples of intergroup behavior:

On ship deck a strolling passenger stops before two other passengers reclining on deck chairs. He admonishes them to stand when he or others like him walk by. The stroller was a missionary returning from Kenya for a furlough in Europe. The action conveyed the respect he, as a European, felt his due from two African students on their way to England (Delf, 1961, p. 74).

Marchers through streets of a city are suddenly attacked by policemen who rain blows on their heads until they fall. Not one marcher raises an arm to protect himself. Those who are missed march silently ahead. This incident occurred during the "Salt March" by the passive resistance movement that followed in the footsteps of Gandhi (Sheean, 1955, p. 159).

At a funeral, a young woman runs up to her father's sister whom she has not seen in several months, greeting her "Hello, auntie!" The older woman tosses her head contemptuously and says, "Don't call me 'auntie.' Call me missus!" According to the official *apartheid* policy in South Africa, the aunt had recently been classified "white." The law required reclassification as "colored" and forfeiture of civil and economic advantages for associating with "coloreds," the legal definition for her niece (*Time*, May 24, 1963, p. 39).

These examples will introduce a central theme of this chapter: the psychology of intergroup attitudes and behaviors must specify contemporary events within the framework of both past relationships between people and their future goals and designs. Otherwise, a large proportion of intergroup actions appears pathological and irrational, as indeed some psychiatrists and social scientists tell us they are.

The Human Past: A Heavy Hand
or Guide to the Future

The past of human experience is distinctive among the living organisms on this planet: it is cumulative, being passed down to new generations through legends, folklore, songs, and sayings as well as codified laws, history books, and other tangible evidences of man's accomplishments and follies. The history of relationships between human groupings forms a large part of this past.

Many of the premises on which members of one grouping base

their notions and treatments of others are rooted in their prior relationships. If a set of people has long been friendly and helpful to us, what more rational premise could we have than to approach and treat them with trust? If, having given aid with strings attached to a less fortunate and less powerful people, we find them appreciative but resentful, it is logical to assume that they appreciated the aid, not the strings. In such instances, the past may be an invaluable guide to future actions.

In this chapter, we consider those psychological effects of the past that interfere with accurate understanding of ongoing events, that hinder formulation of alternatives to the current course of intergroup relationships, and that block attempts toward change in constructive directions.

It runs against the grain of many theorists, psychologists in particular, to include "history" in an analysis of psychological events, such as those traditionally treated under the labels of "group prejudice," "social distance," or "stereotypes." Very few would propose a psychological account that runs counter to historical findings, but some prefer to interpret historical events from a "psychological viewpoint" or to leave historical factors to historians. Of course, historical analysis is the business of historians, not psychologists.

Unfortunately, whether we like it or not, history enters into the very definition of the problem of intergroup attitudes and the images we have of our own and other groups. So long as we ignore the guiding perspective provided by past intergroup relations, formulations on intergroup attitudes will remain contradictory and in some cases erroneous.

This strong assertion can be documented by comparing statements made by leading writers on the topics of group prejudice and stereotypes. The following are representative of popular trends during the last thirty years:

1. Prejudice against other groups and hostile negative images of them invariably accompany the formation of an in-group ("we" feeling). *Not factually true.* Nearly every human group maintains friendly relationships with and correspondingly favorable images of some other groupings. (Berkowitz, 1962, especially 180 ff.; Sherif *et al.*, 1961)

2. Hostile prejudice and unfavorable images are inevitable out-growths of contact between peoples who differ culturally

or physically, the image of the out-group being based on either (a) "outstanding" or (b) "average" types of behavior and traits displayed by members of the other group. *Inadequate.* Both group prejudice and stereotypes can develop between groups whose members differ neither culturally nor physically (see Chapters 5 and 6).

3. Group prejudice and negative stereotypes represent aggressive impulses of individuals displaced toward groupings too weak to retaliate, hence selected as "scapegoats." *Inadequate* (Berkowitz, 1962, especially pp. 135–144). Berkowitz notes that "helpless" groups are not always the objects of hatred, nor the only ones, and that "displacement studies have not yielded consistent results." He concludes that the "scapegoat theory, as usually formulated is incomplete" (p. 141).

4. Stereotyped images of other groups are relied upon more for evaluating "unfamiliar" groups with whom we have little contact. *At least partially wrong.* Results from Katz and Braly's early research in the United States (1933) and from more recent studies in the Near East by Diab (1963a, 1963b) show that the most clear cut and widely shared images were of more familiar groups with significant past and current intergroup relations, such as of Negroes and Jews in the United States, and of Turks and Jews in Lebanon. Least clear cut and consensual images were found for less familiar peoples, for example, Turks in the United States and Chinese in Lebanon.

5. Group stereotypes are "false" or "wrong" concepts of other groups based on inadequate or erroneous information. *Evades the issue of stereotype formation by definition.* The important problem of how group stereotypes originate is solved by denouncing them as "wrong," and attributing their source to lack of adequate information. The basis of group stereotypes is discussed later in this chapter.

6. Negative images of other groups are either (a) "cognitive aspects" of prejudice or (b) "conditioned emotional responses." *Inadequate classifications.* Neither of these contradictory statements clarifies the problem. The former implies that stereotypes, but not attitudes (prejudice) toward other groups, involve human cognition. The latter assumes that they are

acquired through simple associative links with emotional instigators, neglecting the important role of ideational schema.

7. Group prejudice and negative images of other peoples are a function of individual tendencies labeled neurotic or otherwise deviant, usually because of early childhood experiences of severe personal frustration. *Not proven and inadequate* (K. B. Clark, 1955, 68–75; Berkowitz, 1962). The crux of the inadequacy is the lack of a demonstrated relationship between prejudice and no prejudice, on one hand, and neurotic tendencies or childhood frustration, on the other. In a society with discriminatory practices, extreme intensities of prejudice may be related to personal anxieties, including those beginning in childhood. So may lack of prejudice (Hood and Sherif, 1955).

This partial list of the morass of contradictory notions is cited to demonstrate the fundamental weakness of any psychological conception of intergroup attitude and actions that fails to use the background of relationships between human groupings, in the distant and immediate past.

PERSPECTIVE ON INTERGROUP PREJUDICE AND ITS EFFECTS

In one way or another, several of the foregoing notions treat the problem of group prejudice and prevailing images of other groups as though they *originate* in the individual's experiences of frustration, in learning *without* adequate information or *with* emotional arousal, or in particular *psychological* mechanisms. Of course, the individual who detests another group was not born with his hatred. However, the problem of group prejudice and stereotyped images of other groups is not a problem of the idiosyncratic hates and unfounded beliefs of a few separated individuals. It is the problem of hostilities and images shared, in varying degrees, by large numbers of persons belonging to the same human grouping. As Robin Williams has cautioned recently, these persons are not isolated and sealed from one another (1964, p. 361).

Are particular views of other groupings and their members commonly held? What is the background for these views? Answers to these questions are the essential basis for formulating a psychological account of prejudice and stereotypes. Through answering them, we can specify the stimulus situations the individual actually has faced as he comes of age among his "own kind" of people, then study his own attitudes. If this sequence of study is not observed, the penalty is high, both theoretically and practically.

At one time, the view prevailed that group prejudice and unfavorable stereotypes were generated from individual tensions, displacement of individual aggressive tendencies, individual ignorance, individual observation, or experience with members of the despised group. Given such assumptions, it was also reasonable to suppose that the individual phenomena were major *causes* of conflict between human groupings. The practical implication was also logical: attack the problem through correcting misinformation, making individuals aware of the psychological traps into which they had fallen, and treating the emotional complexes.

Going a step further, the more cautious could logically contend that attempts to alter the course of human relationships would fail if the prejudiced attitudes and negative images were not changed first, since these were the roots of the hostile relationships. Most proponents of this conclusion regarded the tasks of education and therapy as requiring at least several generations, hence could see no possibility for early changes in human relationships.

While men of good will pursued the attack on individual attitudes through lecture, pamphlet, and poster, relationships between groupings changed despite prevailing attitudes and images, at times for good and at other times for ill. Stereotyped images of other groups change following altered relationships with those groupings. It is exceedingly difficult to change attitudes when intergroup relationships remain the same, as we shall see (Chapter 5–8). Attitudes toward other groups and images of them are products of particular relationships between groups, not their original cause.

Once this perspective is gained, the acquisition of prejudice by flesh-and-blood persons as they come of age among their "own kind" can be tackled in earnest. Then the effects of attitudes toward others in transactions, negotiations, and struggles with them can be realistically assessed.

Otto Klineberg (1950, 1964) has been prominent among those marshalling evidence that group stereotypes are products, not *initial causes* of rivalry, hostility, and conflicts between peoples. But he further points out that stereotyped images of others do have effects on the course of encounters between individuals who possess them. Indeed, the alternatives a person regards as rational, the way he weighs the evidence, the choices he makes, and his very manner toward members of other groups are affected by his images of them. If the person is a man of great power, his views may affect the course of relationships in irrevocable ways.

Klineberg is supported in this view by a number of political scientists. For example, Robert North (1962) has shown by analyzing the content of historical documents that the way national leaders size up and evaluate the "hard facts" on military and economic capabilities of adversaries, as well as their future intentions, has been affected by the "soft facts" of their preconceptions. Their preconceptions frequently reflect images shared by many others within their own country.

The heavy hand of the past was seen as one contributor to modern wars by a panel of eight social scientists, psychologists, and psychiatrists from seven countries assembled by UNESCO some years ago. Although from diverse backgrounds, they agreed that "myths, traditions, and symbols of national pride handed down from one generation to another" are among the factors conducive to "modern wars between nations and groups of nations" (Cantril, 1950, p. 18).

Thus, group prejudice and derogatory images of other peoples, though products of historical processes forming part of a people's cultural heritage, may exert a fateful influence on the ongoing process between groups. In the context of immediate encounters, the past becomes a heavy hand.

"And Why Do the People Imagine Vain Things?"

This quotation from the Old Testament is preceded by the query "Why do the nations so furiously rage together?" It reflects man's puzzlement throughout the centuries at the apparently unfounded, illogical, or irrational character of human views of peoples other than his own. Certainly this assessment is implicit in many psychological theories of group prejudice and stereotypes, and in the views of many political scientists when they attempt to reckon with the "soft facts" of intergroup and internation struggles.

Human conceptions of and actions toward one another do involve strong emotions. But intense motivations and feelings are involved both when men hate and when they strive together in trust and friendship toward common ends. The label "irrational" hardly clarifies our problem since, thus interpreted, it applies to almost all human transactions.

The semantic trap is avoided by recognizing one fact, documented by history and tested through research: images of other groupings that are widespread and endure over a period of time are invariably formulated from the point of view of the in-group's interests and goals, as parties to the intergroup relationship. Initially, the images are appropriate to *their* position vis à vis the others, or the position they desire to achieve. From the point of view of the people possessing the image, it is rational and logical, given the premise that the others must stand in a certain relationship to them, if they themselves are to attain cherished goals. These images constitute the basis for their ethnocentrism, the tendency to appraise other peoples and events using the values of one's own group as the standards (cf. Campbell and Le Vine, 1961).

The historian Shafer (1955) concluded that a part of the historical process in the rise of modern nation states and nationalistic movements has been the development of conceptions of one's own people that elaborate one's stance relative to others. One's own kind are seen as "kind," "civilized," "progressive." One's representatives in historic events are "heroes" or "martyrs." The opponent is "harsh," "cruel," "backward." His representatives are "zealots." Through history books, folk tales, hero images, poetry, music, and literature, the successes of one's own people are lauded and failures explained, all justified relative to the character of other groupings that have facilitated or impeded them (see especially pp. 184–192).

The singular perspective of one group in historical encounters with others accounts for the "vain" and "illogical" character of standardized group images. This also is the reason why assessing the "truth" or "falsity" in stereotyped views has limited value for understanding their nature or origin. As T. H. Pear, a British psychologist, wrote: *"The world and history cannot be as they appear to the different nations unless we disavow objectivity, reason, and scientific methods of research"* (1950, p. 43, italics in original).

The singular perspective contained in images of a people often appears distorted to individuals belonging to the people so viewed. Nehru (1941) recorded the dilemma of the Indian intellectuals in the late nineteenth century, whose histories "were written entirely from the British imperial viewpoint, and laid stress on our numerous failings in the past and present, and the virtues and high destiny of the British." Like many an oppressed people lacking other sources of information, the Indian intellectuals for some time accepted this viewpoint, finding comfort in their own conclusion that at least they were superior spiritually.

The American Negroes suffered a similar fate for many years and only recently have begun to question the judgment of history as they have learned it, spurred especially by new leadership which has replaced the "accommodating" leaders preceding the civil rights movement (*cf.* Killian, 1962; Killian and Grigg, 1964). Guy B. Johnson foresees greater changes in self images as "net consequences of the abandonment of compulsory segregation." He writes: "I suggest that the greatest positive consequences will be that the white man shall be rid of his false fears and of the stigma of unfair legal compulsion against the Negro, while the Negro shall be rid of a hated symbol of second-class citizenship and a handy alibi for second-rate achievement" (1964, p. 107).

More recently, we learn of a search for *négritude* among several African peoples emerging as nations from the French colonial system. Sometimes conceived of as a spiritual or emotional distinction from whites, the concept appears to be an attempt to find a national identity defined in terms other than those learned in colonial history books. The sociologist Wallerstein (1961) reports that the growth of *négritude* has been led by Africans most thoroughly educated in France and is much less popular in former British colonies. He quotes an African educated in France as saying that the British kept even their educated African subjects at such a clear social distance that they had no *need* for developing a concept of self as African: they had been forced to have one.

ON BECOMING A PERSON WITH A PAST

In less than a decade, a human organism accomplishes a feat otherwise unknown in the animal kingdom. He learns a scheme for classifying all of humanity within the ken of his elders, including many peoples whom they have never seen. There is sex classification, of course, with views of the proper nature and functions of male and female. There are age periods, definitions of kinship varying in kind and degree, stations in life, occupations, religious and political functions, and gradings in all these according to rights, duties, and power. Then there are peoples in other places and locations, some of which the individual will never see himself. In more complex societies, there are diverse ethnic and national groups.

This stupendous accomplishment is expected of a human child in every society. He must master the rudiments of the scheme of social arrangements prevailing around him, at least sufficiently to know *his own* place in them and to behave accordingly from one situation to the next. Slowly, painfully at times, but eagerly, he acquires a knowledge of the range of individual variations in behavior that his elders regard as acceptable in various situations and with different people. Then, over time, he must become able to regulate his own behavior within these acceptable latitudes. Once he does so, his reactions to others no longer exhibit extreme ups-and-downs with the fluctuations of his desire and the vicissitudes of situations, behavior viewed as charming and typical of little children, but alarming and "disturbed" in adults.

Thus, each child in time acquires from his cultural heritage a past in human relationships that becomes *his own*, in the sense that he experiences its facets as his personal tastes, preferences, likes and dislikes and exhibits his unique individuality within socially defined bounds. For many years, this aspect of the socialization process has been dubbed "internalization" of culture.

"INTERNALIZATION" AND LEARNING ABOUT SELF AND OTHERS

The term "internalization" tells us little about what happens, and reflects our appalling ignorance of the psychological process of learning. We do know that it is not only on the order of being "taught" an abstract lesson in a classroom. Indeed, it occurs in a context of other people upon whom the child is dependent for many years for whatever satisfactions he gains for his bodily needs, whatever attachments he develops, whatever love and comfort he experiences. Despite the perennial optimism of some experts on human learning that social learning can be explained through the formation of simple associative links, we know that the part played by simple habit formation or "conditioned" responses, in the classical sense, is probably very minor after the early years of life.

Since the model for classical conditioning studies was developed by Pavlov, whose work is revered by Soviet psychologists, it is appropriate to support this assertion with recent work in the Soviet Union. On the basis of extensive research with human children and cases of brain damage, Luria (1961) writes that the "laws of the formation of temporary links" [that is, conditioned responses] as formulated on the basis of animal experiment are "fundamental . . . beyond doubt. It is noteworthy, however, that none of these applies in full force when we come to analyzing the process of the formation of new temporary links in human beings" (p. 43). "Whereas temporary links evolve gradually in animals, in man they are as a rule formed at once by incorporating the given signal into or excluding it from an existing system of reactions" (pp. 44–45).

The existing system of reactions is "a verbal generalization formulated in inward speech as a hypothetical rule" (p. 44). "This adoption of a verbal rule at once modifies the nature of all subsequent reactions . . . the stimulus in question becomes not a mere signal but *an item of general information,* and all subsequent reactions depend more on the *system* it is taken into than on its physical properties" (p. 44, italics in original).

This perspective on human learning agrees with what is known about the child's formation of stable attitudes toward other people. However, there is another very significant fact: the formation of stable attitudes toward other people, in turn, is part of the process of forming a conception of oneself as a person. The child's earliest intuitions of himself as both subject and object are based on a manifold of sensory-motor-affective experiences during the first year or so of life (cf. Sherif and Cantril, 1947). Sometime during the second or third year as a rule, he acquires words and reveals in the characteristic acceleration of vocabulary growth his general discovery that "things have names." Then the constituents of his self notions are formulated as verbal categories: his name, "I," "you," and later, "boy" or "girl," "we," "us," and "ours."

It is during the early years, around age three, that the child begins to acquire categories for other sets of people who are differentiated by arrangements in his setting from "me" and "us" — his own kind. These categories are not always neutral labels: they define not merely similarities and differences among peoples but the *place* of those people relative to "us," their evaluation along good-bad lines. Later these categories polarize a host of trait adjectives describing *what* those people are like.

This sequence of self-other differentiation and classification is well documented by research summarized in several volumes (for example, Murphy, 1947; Hartley and Hartley, 1952; Allport, 1954; K. B. Clark, 1955; Sherif and Sherif, 1953, 1956). A few generalizations from the research are important for the discussion here.

Differentiation of Self from Others

The process of acquiring categories for self and other people begins with the persons and locations immediately perceivable in the child's surroundings, proceeding outward from his center to conceptions of groupings more remote and more abstract, such as from state to nation, from family to ethnic grouping (*cf.* Hartley, 1946; Piaget and Weil, 1951). But in a society in which the ranking of peoples along scales of superiority-inferiority is salient, group labels with good-bad connotations are evident in children as young as three years (Hartley, 1939; Clark, 1955; Goodman, 1952). In keeping with the more secondary role and lability of linguistic functioning at this age, however, the scheme of invidious categorizations for groups is often employed inconsistently. The child's own place in the scheme is still highly oversimplified. Thus, when asked if she was an American, a little girl of this age replied: "No. My Daddy is. I'm a girl" (Hartley *et al.*, 1948).

By the age of five or six, the child is beginning to regulate his behavior according to verbal rules more consistently and to do so voluntarily (cf. Luria, 1961). With this development, the findings from a variety of studies show a striking convergence that there is increased *consistency* in the child's behavior in a variety of respects. At around this age, consistency in *competing* with others, consistency in *cooperating* with others, consistent expressions of *sympathy* with others, following the *rules* of simple games, and *setting goals* for one's own performance are all reported to appear. And, at this period, the child is able to learn new concepts by formulation of verbal rules. The evidence for these generalizations is reviewed elsewhere (Sherif and Sherif, 1956, Chapters 17, 18).

Henceforth, the categorical places and ranks of other people relative to oneself can be learned *without* direct contact and experience with representatives of those people. In the United States three decades ago, when a scale of invidious social distances was as much an institution as Thanksgiving, Hartley (1936, 1946) and others found that schoolchildren in south, north, east and west, both in rural and urban areas, accepted the prevailing social distances as their own, regardless of prior opportunities for contact with the people in question. The clear exceptions were youngsters whose parents and schools both were making determined efforts to indoctrinate them *not* to discriminate according to group origin.

When there are perceptible differences between peoples, in skin color, dress, or language, it is naturally much easier for a child to achieve the "proper fit" between individuals and social categories. But the perceptible differences are not at all necessary for the child to master a category and behave accordingly to people identified as its members. Many of the social categories are not formulated

on the basis of differences in visibility. Even "racial" identification
in several states is based on proportion of Negro ancestry (one-
eighth in Mississippi), not physical appearance (Silver, 1964).
In forming conceptions of peoples in distant lands, the role of direct
personal experience or differentiating physical differences may be
inconsequential.

IMAGES OF OURSELVES AND OUR
REFERENCE GROUPS

As a general rule, we assess ourselves and our achievements
using a yardstick marked by the accomplishments of others who
count in our eyes. At least a part of the warm glow of experiencing
oneself as a human person is radiated from others with whom we
have ties and frequent give-and-take. Conversely, the icy fingers
of despair grip us most readily when "significant others" are cool,
unappreciative, or harsh. In technical jargon, judgment of self-
accomplishment and self-esteem is closely related to the person's
relationship with his reference groups — those groups or sets of
people to which he belongs or aspires to belong.

The intimate link between our personal elation or disappointment
and the achievement or defeat of our reference groups is revealed
in our emotions when our team competes, our representative nego-
tiates, or when we confront historical symbols and markers of our
people's triumphs or tragedies. It is hardly surprising, then, that
our own groups are usually envisaged in warm and complimentary
terms. Its members are described with favorable, even extravagant
adjectives, such as "noble," "brave," "sturdy," "honest," "heroic."

Cantril and Buchanan (1953) compared the adjectives used by
most persons in representative cross-sections of nine European and
American countries to describe their own nationalities. They found
them almost entirely favorable. When the German psychologist
Peter Hofstätter (1957) correlated the responses in one country
with those in each of the others, he found very high correspondence
between the images people in different countries held of their own
countries.

In view of the autistic tendency to see oneself and one's own
actions in as favorable a light as possible, we might regard the self-
glorifying images of our own groups as psychologically inevitable.
The fact that this is *not* invariably the case tells us something
significant about the origins of the images we hold of our own
groups and of other groups.

Social Arrangements, Social Distances,
and Group Images

When human groupings live in arrangements of domination and subordination, the dominant groupings control the major facets of living, the opportunities, and level of achievements available to others. The ordering of prestige among the various groupings, the social intimacy or distance permitted and deemed desirable between them, and the prevailing images flow from the powerful and mighty downward to the subordinated.

In such contexts, it is not unusual for dominated groups to be hostile and prejudiced against the very same groups as their masters. Their images of themselves may reflect some of the unfavorable evaluation placed upon them by others, amounting almost to self-hatred at times. Similarly, in the context of a deadly struggle between groups and peoples, the defeated parties may accept, at least temporarily, the verdict of the victors as to their inferior qualities and internal weaknesses that led to defeat.

For many years, the rankings of ethnic and national groups in the United States changed very little upon a scale of social distances, which denoted the degree of intimacy or estrangement regarded as desirable between one's own group and others (Bogardus, 1928, 1947). The ranking of groups on the social distance scale was virtually the same for members of the dominant white Protestants and for members of groups in lower and subordinate ranks, with one striking exception (Hartley, 1946). Negroes and members of other groups of low standing would move their own group from its lowly position up nearer the top.

Along with the social arrangements prohibiting or inhibiting equality of opportunity, curtailing contact between groups, and fostering invidious comparisons, research in the United States revealed a remarkable consensus on the "traits" describing each of the ethnic or national groups. Social scientists and psychologists studying the clusters of adjectives that were used to describe these groups called them "stereotypes," a term used by the political commentator Walter Lippmann in his early book *Public Opinion* (1922). In terms of research operations, *a group stereotype may be said to exist when a large proportion within a group agree, over a period of time, that a particular cluster of adjectives describes all or most members of a human classification.*

In general, the labels and adjectives describing powerful strata in society or the powerful nations from which they originally came were laudatory and favorable (for example, Great Britain). Going downward in social rank, the favorable adjectives declined amidst an increasing proliferation of critical and unflattering trait names. The pattern of traits attributed to groups at the very bottom was so derogatory as to scarcely describe human beings.

Only a few decades ago, members of the lowly placed, including Negro college students (Meenes, 1943), sometimes accepted the deprecatory images of their own groups as well as the stereotyped descriptions of other groups on the social distance scale. A similar phenomenon was reported by G. Jahoda (1961) in the Gold Coast before independence, where native school children frequently described natives in the derogatory and Europeans in the admiring terms used by children of the European colonialist.

It is easy enough, having made discoveries such as these, to regard "stereotypes" as "pictures in our heads" having only psychic reality and support. But, as Frazier (1957) pointed out, the Negro did not need to be told he was socially inferior, nor did the white child have to imagine it. The fact was evident in all walks of life through the absence of Negroes from positions of power and prestige and the presence of whites in those positions.

For the Negro child and for the white child, the definition of themselves as belonging to socially superior or inferior categories is an early realization. Ruth Hartley (1939) and the Clarks (1955) have documented the tragic ambivalence of Negro pre-school children in identifying themselves as Negro, and the certainty of the white child's choice of a white image. The location of one's image as desirable or undesirable is not the equivalent of a full-blown image of all the attributes one is supposed to possess, however. In fact, Blake and Dennis (1943) found that in the early elementary grades, white Southern children attributed all the unfavorable adjectives to Negroes, whereas the more specific cluster composing the adult stereotype appeared in the later elementary grades, including as it did a few "redeeming" features in American terms (such as "religious" and "musical").

Research seems to indicate that young children in the United States and the Soviet Union today hold images of their own and the other nation that represent "mirror images" (cf. Bronfenbrenner, 1961; White, 1961; Osgood, 1962). It must be said that these images reflect the social arrangements around them quite as much as deliberate indoctrination by adults. How could a child logically account for the prominence of military service, weapons, and rockets if there were no real or potential "enemy?" The consensus found among adults on specific characteristics attributed to themselves and to other peoples is not accomplished without some support from existing social arrangements.

GROUP STEREOTYPES IN THE CONTEXT
OF CHANGING INTERGROUP RELATIONS

In studying oxygen metabolism, it is considered good scientific procedure to vary the oxygen concentration in the atmosphere. Similarly, changes in intergroup relations reveal more about the bases of group stereotypes than a constant environment. The world today is not lacking in changes, though in many cases the currents are too new to foresee their consequences.

Certainly, we are witnessing changes in the United States in relationships between white and Negro citizens. Already, we are told by experts on Negro youth (Frazier, 1957; Jones, 1965) that many young people are rejecting the traditionally unfavorable images of their own groups and affirming their rights to human dignity.

The changes are not an outgrowth of widespread reversals in the attitudes of white Americans, although such changes have been noted for many years, especially since World War II. They owe quite as much to the pressures on official America to gain or keep a favorable image in a world with a large population with colored skins. From desegregation of the military services to the 1964 civil rights legislation, official steps have proceeded from the most powerful segments of official society, with or without the assent of the populace involved. In fact, Killian (1962) reports very low correlations between active resistance to desegregation and prejudiced attitudes of the residents in the so-called border states.

Those who see the actual events of intergroup relations and stereotyped images as two entirely separate spheres may profitably recall that stereotyped images of Negro Americans have already changed, notably during the nineteenth century. By analyzing newspapers, literature, songs, and cartoons, Goldstein (1948) showed that the unfavorable images of the Negro varied during the course of Negro-white relations even within the prevailing doctrine of racism, which was the ideological bulwark for perpetuating white dominance.

The image of the happy Negro slave grew after about 1820. The timing of this image with the growth of abolitionism in the North and more than two hundred documented slave uprisings in the

South (cf. Rose, 1948) is ironic, but not paradoxical from the viewpoint of the slave-owners' interests. With the freeing of the slaves after the Civil War, the hitherto gentle and contented Negro became a "brute," endowed with uncontrollable animal instincts endangering, especially, white women. Still later, the comic figure developed who attempted a crude imitation of "white folks'" ways and possessions. What a strange sequence of images this is, if one is not familiar with the changes that preceded and accompanied them.

A reverse sequence is reported by Wertheim (1956) for the Dutch image of Indonesians, the alterations coinciding with the conquest and subjugation of the people. At the start of the nineteenth century, the Javanese were still engaged in "continuous warfare" against the colonialists and were described as fierce, warlike, and violent. The subduing of resistance was followed, around 1900, by an officially endorsed image of the Indonesians as calm, gentle, pliable, and meek.

Commenting on the drastic changes in the image of Chinese immigrants in California during a much shorter period bridging the Civil War, Klineberg (1950) concluded that the only acceptable explanation for the astonishing change was that it became "advantageous for the whites to eliminate the Chinese from economic competition," whereas their services had previously been sorely needed. Changes in both the economic relationship to native Africans and ideological content were seen by MacCrone (1937) as the antecedents of the altered picture of the native by Europeans in South Africa, from that of "heathen" to that of the inferior to "white man and his civilization."

The critical importance of actual relations between groups in the choice of stereotyped traits was illustrated more recently by Zaidi and Ahmed (1958) through comparison of Pakistani's views of Americans and British. In East Pakistan, where the British first consolidated their power in India (Bengal), the British were viewed as aggressive, conservative, and cunning, while the Americans were considered friendly, generous, and open-minded. In West Pakistan, there had been more direct contact with Americans since the War, and less previous contact with the British than in East Pakistan. In the West, the image of the British was favorable (intelligent, hardworking, and clean), but the image of Americans was tarnished by the substitution of "cheats" for "clean." (The actual term was "420," the number of the Criminal Code article dealing with cheating.)

In the United States, it is well known that both the social-distance ranks and the stereotypes attributed to various countries changed during World War II, according to whether the country in question was an enemy (Japan, Germany) or an ally (China, Russia). Since the advent of the "Cold War," there have been numerous reports of extremely negative images of Russians in the United States and of Americans in the Soviet Union. There have been efforts on both sides to apply the images to the opposition government, rather than the people, but the success of such efforts has not been assessed.

THE NATURE OF INTERGROUP ATTITUDES AND STEREOTYPES

A characterization of intergroup attitudes and images will now be proposed as a guide for future research. It is based on a survey of research findings, of which those in this chapter are illustrative.

An intergroup attitude may be defined as a set of categories (as may any social attitude) within which a person belonging to one group locates other people as similar-dissimilar to himself and evaluates these similarities-differences as acceptable or unacceptable to him in some degree (cf. Sherif, Sherif, and Nebergall, 1965). His attitude is formed (acquired) as he interacts with others who count in his eyes. Thus it is affected by norms or shared images (stereotypes) prevailing within the groups in which he actually moves or to which he urgently desires to belong, and by the ongoing transactions between his groups and other groups. Even if the content of an intergroup attitude stems exclusively from mass media of communication, its formation by the person presupposes that he accepts the content as defining or elaborating his concept of himself and "his kind" in relation to other categories of people.

Once a grouping of people is classified positively or negatively relative to one's own, the conception of that group is elaborated by a host of traits, attributes, and beliefs about the people in that group. The attributes, typically expressed through descriptive adjectives or labels, are patterned within the favorable or unfavorable category in which the group is located, relative to one's own group. The choice and the salience of particular attributes in the pattern reflect the stance of our own group in past and/or current relationships with the particular group in question. Both the generalized and vague descriptive character of the attributes and their singular point of view make the search for "kernels of truth" in stereotypes unrewarding.

The concept of "group stereotypes" is useful only when it can be shown that a particular image (pattern of attributes) is attributed by a significant segment of one group to another. The criteria for agreement and for size of the segment must be determined according to the problem being studied, but they should certainly be based on the power and prestige of the segment in question as well as sheer numbers. In other usages, the term "stereotype," with its usual connotations of "fixed," "unalterable," "automatic," is positively misleading for understanding the phenomena in question.

From this characterization, it is clear that intergroup attitudes and stereotypes are by no means confined to relationships between religious, ethnic, racial, or national groups. Prejudice (which is simply a special label for a hostile and unfavorable intergroup attitude) and derogatory images are well documented between various groups in which cultural or national differences play little or no part. Clemmer (1940) reported clear cut prejudice and stereotypes among prisoners toward guards and other prison authorities. Juvenile gangs attribute highly standardized traits to other groups and to adults, including the police (Sherif and Sherif, 1964). Cases of standardized and derogatory images held by union officers of management (cold, manipulating, overbearing, deceitful) and by management of union officers (stupid, unintelligent, disloyal) have been documented once more by Blake, Shepard, and Mouton (1964, pp. 40, 173). The distinctive character of prejudice and stereotypes directed toward underprivileged ethnic or national groups is not that they exist but that they are buttressed by doctrines of racial inferiority.

INTERGROUP ATTITUDES AND CATEGORICAL PROCESSES

Research inventories of how groups and nations view one another overflow the literature on intergroup attitudes. The theoretical and practical value of further research that merely documents the traits attributed by various peoples to others is doubtful. It is known already that intergroup image can be predicted fairly accurately simply from the course of dealings between the groups. In general, nice words are reserved for ourselves and our friends, and nasty words are reserved for those seen as threatening or as enemies, even when referring to the same actions.

A more fruitful emphasis would be the relevance of categorical thought and judgment for theory and research on intergroup attitudes (cf. Allport, 1954, Chapter 2). The suggestion is not novel, but it has failed to lead to systematic research and has fostered certain misleading conclusions.

It is one thing to assert that the psychological processes whereby men come to view one another as friend or foe are rooted in man's capacities to learn according to generalized verbal categories and rules. It would be quite another to conclude that this human capacity is in any way "to blame" for hostile prejudices and stereotypes. Within the context of established or developing dominance-subordination and conflicts of vital interests, human categorizations take on different content.

The categories for human groupings that prevail among many of the large and powerful peoples of the world today are not identical to just any other linguistic category. They incorporate an ingrained ideational heritage concerning the nature of human beings. Attributes used to describe people are considered as *essences* of the people in that category, rather than terms ascribed to them or describing our judgments about them. Women are "by nature" impractical; members of that family have "always" been cunning, so "what do you expect of *him?*"

This ideational heritage for categorization of peoples deals with *substances*, as though a person possessed an unvarying quantity of *something*, regardless of time and circumstances. Its most vicious and untenable form is racist doctrine, explaining and justifying social inequality in terms of the inherent, hence unchangeable biological superiority of some people over others. The doctrine is untenable because it cannot be proven and because available evidence to the contrary has been marshaled by the leading geneticists, psychologists, and anthropologists of the entire world (Tumin, 1963).

The racist doctrine still pervades much of the categorical thought of large populations in the world today. At times it is masked in terms of a "white man's civilization" that can be understood and appreciated only by those born into its bosom. Much of the stereotyped fare on American television programs is incomprehensible without tacit racist assumptions: one thinks of an evening during which a "sophisticated" comic draws roars with a joke about the dangers of cannibalism in a newly independent African country, followed by a movie showing wholesale slaughter of American Indians by heroic troops, a news report calmly detailing destruction of an Asian village and the bombing of a Negro church.

Any analysis of categorical thinking and judgment in intergroup relations must necessarily consider the ideational content, especially the substantive and racist doctrines. Then, categorical thought has definite bearing on intergroup attitudes and social processes between groups. The considerable body of facts about categorical judgment, for example, is directly pertinent to studies of the behavioral effects of group stereotypes. Some examples may be cited.

Categorical Judgment and Effects of Group Stereotypes

When a person appraises an object or another person, he must have something to compare it with. One of the most general and well established principles in psychology is that the particular standard chosen has definite effects upon the judgment a person gives. Among these effects are the heightening of similarities between the standard and neighboring items (whether these be weights, lines, or sound intensities) and the exaggeration of differences from the standard. It is said, then, that the standard "anchors" our appraisal of other objects.

Now, let us consider the case in which the standard represents something very dear to us, something in which we are personally involved to the point that it is part of us. When we are then judging others by this standard, the well-known phenomena of incorporating similar things to the standard (*assimilation*) and displacing dissimilar items away from it (*contrast*) are striking (cf. Sherif and Hovland, 1961; Sherif, Sherif, and Nebergall, 1965). They may become so pronounced that *all* other views, all other people and their characteristics are either like the standard or unlike it. This phenomenon is exemplified in the phrase, "Those who are not for us are against us."

Many of the effects of group stereotypes found in the research literature can be handled within these and closely related principles of categorical judgment. For example, in judging the character of other people whom we like very much or dislike heartily, our appraisal depends in part upon whom we are comparing. Compared to ourselves alone, even friendly groups are seen as less desirable than when we also consider others who are not favorably regarded (Sherif, 1961). Or, if we compare just a few groups, all of which we dislike, the characteristics of the least detested are more favorable than is otherwise the case (Diab, 1963a, 1963b).

Once placed into an acceptable or unacceptable category, however, there is a tendency to view any member of a group as similar to any other in the category. Thus, once categorized as Negro, pictures of Negro faces call forth to the prejudiced person all the unfavorable personal qualities that go with the category, even though the faces vary markedly in Negroid features (Secord, Bevan, and Katz, 1956). Once categorized in a favorable or unfavorable pigeonhole, we perceive, quite selectively of course, the traits attributed to that pigeonhole (Razran, 1950). On objective tests of familiar material, we recognize our own viewpoints more readily and fail to see our similarities with those whom we have placed at an unfavorable distance from ourselves as rivals or antagonists (Blake, Shepard, and Mouton, 1964). In remembering events about people, our memory "plays tricks," for it reconstructs actions and appearances to fit the favorable or unfavorable image into which we cast the people (Allport and Postman, 1947).

The more closely we cling to ourselves, our kind, and our views as the standards, the fewer categories we need to sort out and appraise the myriad other persons, groups, and views (Sherif and Sherif, 1965). The more important the characteristic we are appraising, the more likely we are to make extreme judgments, amounting to a two-valued ruler (Tajfel and Wilkes, 1964).

In those matters most near and dear to us, our particular location in the spectrum becomes the sole anchor by which to assess all others. Thus, the white ministers of Birmingham saw Martin Luther King's course there as "extreme," while he himself concluded that he was a moderate compared to either their views or those of a rising "black nationalism" (King, 1964). The "moderate" in a political struggle is successively seen by both sides as giving comfort to the opposition. The "neutral" or "unaligned" nation is constantly suspect to the aligned, who see each interchange with the opposition as alignment.

In Chapters 5 to 7, further effects of intergroup attitudes and derogatory images will be explored.

The next chapter inquires into the springs of hostility or affection that lead to categorization of a whole people as admirable or detestable.

3

Doctrine and Fact on the Psychological Springs of Aggression

When persons belonging to one human grouping are dead set against people in another, they are moved passionately towards fulfillment of what they feel as an urgent mission that is irrevocable in the hearts of all who are true and worthy. They are stirred more profoundly than by the daily routine of their business, their everyday likes and dislikes, or the pleasures and jealousies of their daily person-to-person encounters. They are moved by an infallible sense of the righteousness of the place they claim in the sun and the justice of their course. The adversary is the wicked, malicious, and greedy source of ill will and conflict.

No one can deny that men's inhumanity, aggressiveness, and vindictiveness to men are instigated by strong emotions. This is not at issue. The great question is how the aggressive, destructive feelings are generated.

What are the springs of the emotions that individuals experience toward other peoples? There is still confusion concerning this fundamental question, but not because great writers have failed to tackle it. Psychologists, political philosophers, and other com-

42

mentators on human relations have offered answers. Then why
is there still no answer satisfactory even to experts? We are just
beginning to realize the source of the difficulty. The nature of
cooperativeness or competitiveness, compassion or aggressiveness,
creativeness or destructiveness in human relations has been described in the image of the groups in which the particular author
is a committed member.

An adequate framework for social psychological formulation on
the rise of intergroup emotions as instigators of deeds is a compara-
tively recent development. Early psychological experiments bearing on the etiology of intergroup feelings were fragmentary and
frequently off the mark, largely because they failed to define the
variables that distinguish the domain of intergroup relations from
that of interpersonal relations.

In this chapter, we shall look more closely at important doctrines about feelings, emotions, and attitudes prompting intergroup
action, for good or evil. Research and critical evaluations of accumulating research are so recent that they are just beginning to
be incorporated into textbooks and other readily available media.
The modern trend will be better articulated after we glance in this
chapter at major theories which received such wide circulation that
they were assumed as premises in evaluating intergroup events.

AGGRESSION IN HUMAN RELATIONS
AND MAN'S NATURE

In accounting for aggression or cooperation in human relations,
traditional theorizing falls into two main camps, each with variations on its theme: the instinctivist camp and the environmentalist
camp.

The instinctivist camp explained the state of human relations
in terms of primordial dispositions inhering in human nature. These
dispositions, it was suggested, seek releasers that have no function
other than to trigger an eruption. Thus, Hobbes depicted a human
nature that is selfish, sneaky, and aggressive. Rousseau, disgusted
by human relations in the hands of a degenerate and decaying
aristocracy, depicted human nature as essentially innocent and
good, but distorted by the shackles of the corrupt social order of
his age. The environmentalist camp, on the other hand, put the
praise or blame for human relations entirely on the cultural, social,
political, and economic conditions surrounding men.

In our view, both the instinctivist position and the wholly environmentalist position give mutilated pictures of human motives and ambitions, especially as humans transact in group units. An adequate account of man's motives and ambitions as instigators of deeds in human relations can start only by relating his goals and designs to his membership in human groupings under the circumstances of their concrete environments. This environment includes other human groupings with which he and his groups interact.

Until very recently, the most influential psychological theories have tenaciously put the blame for destruction and murder committed by human groups on destructive and aggressive dispositions inherent in human nature. For example, one well-known list of innate dispositions was posited by William McDougall. McDougall (1923) included in his list the instincts of ascendance and submission, along with instincts of pugnacity and acquisition.

The "instinctive" terms included in such lists have varied according to the social philosophy and pessimistic or optimistic outlook of the authors themselves. The presence or absence of aggressive dispositions is one index of the conception of human relations held in given societies or by particular authors. According to its social arrangements, each society has its "myth" about the Nature of Man, as cogently noted by Tolman. Being a peace-loving man in a war-torn world, Tolman (1942) included "loyalty to the group" and "sharing" in his own list of social drives.

"Death Instinct"

The instinctivist position explains the destruction of men by men and the vindictiveness of group toward group on the basis of blind aggressive forces erupting from the depths of human nature. Perhaps its most influential proponent has been Sigmund Freud, the towering figure of the psychoanalytic movement. In his earlier work, Freud saw aggression as a response to the frustration of impulses that he then conceived as more basic. In his later writings, he posited an "innate, independent, instinctual disposition in man" toward aggression (1930, p. 102). Specifically, when problems of group relations became of greater concern to him, he developed the notion of two classes of instincts: "Eros or the sexual instincts" and a "death instinct, the task of which is to lead organic matter back into the inorganic state" (1927, p. 55).

For Freud, it was Eros that held human beings together in

groups, but Eros was easily ravaged by the onslaughts of aggressive impulses of the death instinct. Freud was very explicit on this point:

> This aggressive cruelty usually lies in wait of some provocation, or else it steps into the service of some other purpose, the aim of which might as well have been achieved by milder measures. . . . It also manifests itself spontaneously and reveals men as savage beasts to whom the thought of sparing their own kind is alien. . . . The existence of this tendency for aggression . . . makes it necessary for culture to institute its high demands. Civilized society is perpetually menaced with disintegration through this primary hostility of men towards one another (1930, pp. 85–86).

Thus, the ultimate reason for the existence of human culture as well as its greatest threat are seen in man's innate destructiveness. Society, in Freud's eyes, was an inevitable enemy of the individual. The individual conscience was essentially "dread of society" (1922, p. 10).

In his chapter "The Psychological Study of Tensions and Conflict" for *The Nature of Conflict* (1957), published for UNESCO (United Nations Educational, Scientific and Cultural Organization), T. H. Pear summarizes Freud's position on innate aggressive impulses along the same lines. Earlier, Pear had commented that Freud's "one-sided, pessimistic view of society is related to the fact that he wrote in a particular setting" and developed his ideas of human aggressiveness and hatred "during the most depressing time in Vienna" (Pear, 1950, p. 40).

For Freud, interaction in groups and collective encounters did not produce creative outcomes. On the contrary, they served only to release man's instinctive impulses:

> From our point of view we need not attribute so much importance to the appearance of new characteristics. For us it would be enough to say that in a group the individual is brought under conditions which allow him to throw off the repressions of his unconscious instincts. The apparently new characteristics which he then displays are in fact the manifestation of his unconscious, in which all that is evil in the human mind is contained as a pre-disposition (1922, pp. 9–10).

Freud's contention is, of course, in sharp opposition to results obtained in research on social interaction by social scientists during the last thirty years. Chapters 5 and 6 present research evidence that unmistakably demonstrates the impact of interaction in groups, even to the extent of recasting the motives and attitudes of participants.

RECENT CRITIQUE OF DOCTRINE OF AGGRESSIVE INSTINCTS

All of us, psychologists and laymen alike, seem irresistibly fascinated with musing over ourselves, our desires, our attachments and fantasies when we were children and adolescents with kaleidoscopic dreams. There is fascination in abandoning the usual restrictions and revealing ourselves freely to a trusted friend, to a beloved person, or in the permissive atmosphere of a confessional or therapeutic session.

The range of conscious awareness is very limited, as so many studies have established. The happenings of our past are inseparable parts of our self-identity, whether they are horrid or pleasant, whether the source of our guilt, shame, inner conflict, or gratification. Beset with tedious preoccupations and role conflicts in a modern life that is casually, even contradictorily patterned, we develop a craving to unearth those parts of ourselves hidden by the limited awareness of the living present. This fascination may be partially responsible for the appeal of dramatic accounts of unbridled impulses lying beneath conscious awareness, such as presented in the aggression doctrine under consideration.

The doctrine of all-powerful aggressive impulses inhering in a "death instinct" had its critics even in the heyday of the psychoanalytic movement. Critics appeared both within the fold of the movement and outside it. Our concern with psychoanalytic theory in this book is restricted to the doctrine of aggressive impulse, which is assumed to appear when the brakes are not sufficiently strong and to flare up in collective interaction situations. It is beyond the scope of this book to survey Freudian theory or its modern versions in other respects, for example, on the nature of the unconscious, of repression, and other psychoanalytic mechanisms.

Experimental, developmental, and other research evidence on intergroup attitudes and deeds has made increasingly untenable the explanation of aggression in human relations on the basis of innate impulses originating in an all-powerful death instinct.

Berkowitz, in his comprehensive survey on aggression, brings a great deal of coherence to the problem area. He presents theories of aggression and critically evaluates them in the light of available research findings from diverse disciplines. His concise critical statement of the doctrine of an innate death instinct is worth noting:

> Freud and his disciples regarded hostile actions as impelled by a constantly driving force (i.e., the causal condition is entirely within the organism) whose energy must be released in one manner or another. Freud believed this energy stems from the "death instinct," a fundamental tendency to return to the quiescence of inorganic matter supposedly inherent in all living organisms. Impulses toward self-destruction motivating the individual to kill himself will arise as he seeks the elimination of internal stimulation, according to this conception, but the self-destruction is prevented by the turning outward of the aggressive impulses. Attacks upon others, either directly or in substitute form as attempts to control or master others, are said to provide an outlet for the energy of the death instinct.
>
> Research findings offer little support for this reasoning. A wide variety of studies demonstrate that not all animal behavior is oriented toward tension reduction. Human beings as well as lower animals frequently work for an increase in internal excitations, indicating that organisms desire an optimal level of stimulation, and perhaps occasional variations in this level, but not the complete elimination of excitation (1962, pp. 23–24).

Berkowitz' conclusion is that

> very few psychoanalysts today accept Freud's hypothesis of a death instinct. Dramatic though it may be, the concept of an innate drive for destruction, as Freud posited it, is scientifically unwarranted. . . . There are a number of bases upon which the hypothesis can be attacked, some logical, others factual (p. 8).

The Error of Attributing Man's Aggression to Animal Nature

Another lingering misconception is the postulation of a fighting impulse inherent in biological organisms. This misconception seems to arise from the undeniable fact that frequent fights occur among some species of animals. A fighting instinct has been postulated without detailed examination of the causes of these fights. On the basis of long years of systematic studies of animals, J. P. Scott reached the following conclusion:

> The important fact is that the chain of causation in every case eventually traces back to the outside. There is no physiological evidence of any spontaneous stimulation for fighting arising within the body. This means that there is no need for fighting, either aggressive or defensive, apart from what happens in the external environment. We may conclude that a person who is fortunate enough to exist in an environment which is without stimulation to fight will not suffer physiological or nervous damage because he never fights. This is a quite different situation from the physiology of eating, where the internal processes of metabolism lead to definite physiological changes which eventually produce hunger and stimulation to eat, without any change in the external environment (1958, p. 62).

The entire concept of animal "instinct" is being subjected to searching examination today in the light of recent research (cf. Schneirla, 1964). Much animal behavior that was called "instinctive" because it occurred with relative invariance among members of a species turns out to involve a complex learning process by organisms developing in particular environments and with species-specific capacities for perception, locomotion, and so on.

As Schneirla has demonstrated in a series of penetrating analyses, the criteria for drawing valid analogies between animal behavior and human behavior cannot rest solely on similarity of outcomes (e.g., injury to another), or complexity of performance (witness the army ant's maneuvers), or degree of adaptation to the environment. The criteria for proper analogies between behavior of different species must be found in the comparability of the *processes* underlying the behavior (Schneirla, 1946, 1951, 1953).

As noted in the last chapter, accounts of human aggressiveness must include the process, specific to the human species, by which man learns and responds to external stimulation in accordance with verbally formulated rules or generalizations. Because of this process, man's aggression to man does not vary systematically according to the same conditions, such as food shortages and ecological arrangements, as it does in lower species. On the contrary, the most violent acts of human aggression seem to involve individuals and groups with greater food supplies, more space, and greater facilities for adaptation without aggression.

Error of Generalizing from Atypical Populations

Probably one reason that a self-generated instinct of aggression was postulated by psychoanalysts is that they based their theorizing on a select sample of individuals — disturbed, deranged, at odds with their fellow men. We borrow this inference from a leading researcher on human development, Robert R. Sears (1960), who spent years studying children in their friendly and hostile interpersonal relations. In an eye-opening chapter entitled "The Growth of Conscience," Sears draws attention to the pitfall of making wholesale inferences from data on a select and unrepresentative sample:

> I think it is not surprising that the first two aspects of conscience [resistance to temptation and guilt] have been more studied than the third and more positive one. Much of what we know — or at least hypothesize — about the moral properties of human behavior comes from the clinic. Only recently have more experimental and more replicable investigations begun to examine these matters. Quite naturally, such studies have begun with the clinically obtained hypotheses. And clearly, the clinic historically has drawn its main clientele from the ill, the disturbed, the badly socialized. These are the ones who resist temptation too little or too much, and who are in trouble one way or another with their feelings of guilt. A clinic population does not draw so heavily from those who are achieving their own ideals. Even among the ill, the therapeutic focus seems to fall more intensively on lapses from grace than on failures to achieve the ideal (1960, p. 96).

A select sample of clinical cases, who admittedly are at odds with their fellow men, is not the only source of uncritical assumptions concerning the basic friendliness or vindictiveness of human motivation. There is a related habit, hard to overcome because it is so strongly ingrained. The tendency is to jump to conclusions and to evaluate human beings everywhere on the basis of the standards

of value inculcated in us within the confines of human arrangements prevailing in our own culture (Chapter 2). This habit is
responsible for many of our ethnocentric generalizations on human
affairs, so characteristic of a "closed mind" depicted in detail by
Rokeach (1960).

Although modern anthropology has fully documented the wide
variations in competition, submission, and aggression in different
cultures, some psychological research on these topics proceeds
uncritically from assumptions unwarranted by anthropological evidence. For this reason, some generalizations about aggressiveness
in social transactions made by students of the evolution of human
culture are highly instructive.

The Error in Seeking the Roots
of Aggressiveness in Primitive
Cultures

In theorizing about human nature, it has been almost an article
of faith that the pristine traits of humanity would be revealed more
clearly among peoples in more primitive cultures. Technically
developed societies should be further removed from original human
impulses, according to this reasoning. Therefore, if one would
know whether human nature is innately aggressive, look to man
in a less developed society.

Especially since the latter half of the nineteenth century, treatises
marshaling evidence from various primitive cultures have been
written in efforts to prove the particular author's assumptions about
the traits of original human nature. The selectivity of the cases
included by various authors, in line with their particular assumptions, is a fascinating example of the intrusion of subjective factors
in shaping discrimination and decision, which has also been found
in a number of laboratory experiments.

Psychological theorizing on influences contributing to friendship
or enmity between human groups gains perspective if it starts
from the vantage point provided by cultural anthropology as to
the occurrence, frequency, and scope of friendly or hostile intergroup events. Especially helpful for the student of intergroup
relations is the orientation pursued for years by Leslie White and
his associates. White and his associates do not present psychological analyses; on the contrary, they provide a notion of culture
at its own *level* of organization. The conception of culture is not
reductionistic; culture is not reduced to unrelated, meaningless bits

of behavior with no context. Culture is conceived of as a meaningful structure. From a psychological viewpoint, relevant aspects of this pattern are parts of the stimulus world the individual confronts. His perceptions can be assessed more effectively within this cultural context.

A distinctive feature of White's orientation makes it particularly pertinent for assessing the human and physical arrangements contributing to positive or negative relations between human groupings. Instead of considering each cultural group as a more or less closed "culture pattern," each a law virtually unto itself, this orientation puts cultures in a *time* perspective. Lawful recurrences over time enable comparisons between cultures at different times, in terms of the actualities of prevailing conditions, techniques, modes of life, and premises regulating human arrangements (e.g., White, 1959).

Working within the orientation of cultural evolution, Marshall D. Sahlins (1960) in a paper on the "Origin of Society" reached a conclusion about the search for the roots of aggression in primitive societies. It should serve as a corrective to statements about original human impulses formulated without regard to the prevailing mode of life and human arrangements:

> Territorial relations among neighboring human hunting-and-gathering bands (a term used technically to refer to the cohesive local group) offer an instructive contrast. The band territory is never exclusive. . . . Warfare is limited among hunters and gatherers. Indeed, many are reported to find the idea of war incomprehensible. A massive military effort would be difficult to sustain for technical and logistic reasons. But war is even further inhibited by the spread of a social relation — kinship — which in primitive society is often a synonym for "peace." Thomas Hobbes' famous fantasy of a war of "all against all" in the natural state could not be further from the truth. War increases in intensity, bloodiness, duration and significance for social survival through the evolution of culture, reaching its culmination in modern civilization. Paradoxically the cruel belligerence that is popularly considered the epitome of human nature reaches its zenith in the human condition most removed from the pristine. By contrast, it has been remarked of the Bushmen that "it is not in their nature to fight" (1960, pp. 81–82).

Human Motives and Their
Social Context

Early in this century, theory in academic psychology was primarily intellectualistic. Reacting against this heritage, the emphasis shifted toward the psychodynamics of instinctual impulses conceived of as the driving force of man's deeds, even though he is not aware of them. Reaction against the over-intellectualistic tradition was carried too far. In some quarters, emphasis on the vicissitudes of instincts is still very much alive. In others, motivational forces, even acquired motives, are taken as absolute determinants of behavior. An impressive series of assertions by well-known therapists and other psychodynamicists could be quoted to document the excessive emphasis on motives, an overemphasis that runs contrary to the converging trend reported in this chapter.

As Eysenck stated:

> In their excitement about the discovery of the powers of "emotion" over "intellect," many psychologists have gone to extremes, portraying the "man in the street" as the mere plaything of uncontrollable unconscious forces which cannot in any way be influenced by reason. Such a view is no less contrary to fact than the previous overestimation of rationalistic influences; what is needed is a more realistic appraisal of the relative importance of these two factors in each individual case (1950, p. 64).

If we have any pretense of a scientific approach, we must heed the indications of converging lines from psychiatry, studies of human development, animal studies, social psychology, and cultural anthropology. Contrary to these indications, the psychodynamicists have tended to view the individual as a self-contained powerhouse, generating his own impulses without regard to transactions with his cultural setting; to view the development of human conscience as merely the "dread of society"; to view society itself solely as the agent of oppression to the individual's impulses and passions. A balanced view must consider society as more than a system of suppressive prohibitions and conscience as more than "dread of society," but also composed of the values and imperatives of social groups of which the individual is an integral part (cf. Pear, 1950, p. 134).

Because of past emphases, a social scientist is still expected to be an apologist for the group or culture, and the psychiatrist and psychologist partial to psychodynamic explanations, ignoring group and social influences. Developments in recent theory and research are eliminating the one-sided emphasis in both social science and psychology. The adequate study of man and his relations requires taking into account his intimately felt motives, yearnings, aspirations, and the workings of his cognition in the context of his affiliations with other people and the sociocultural setting of which he is a part (Sherif and Koslin, 1960; Sherif and Sherif, 1964). No man feels, yearns, thinks, hates, or fights altogether in isolation.

What is uniquely individual and what is sociocultural must be integrated in the study of man's relation to man, including his aggressive confrontations. This view has gained substantial support in recent years, factually and theoretically. A recent expression is found in a monograph on "Psychiatric Aspects of the Prevention of Nuclear War" prepared by the Group for the Advancement of Psychiatry (1964). After reviewing a considerable body of relevant material the authors recapitulate their conclusion:

> War is a social institution; it is not inevitably rooted in the nature of man. Although war has traditionally served as an outlet for many basic human psychological needs, both aggressive and socially cohesive ones, the increasing mechanization and automation of modern warfare has rendered it less and less relevant to these needs. There are other social institutions and other means of conducting conflict between groups of people, or between nations, that can serve these psychological needs more adaptively in our modern world.
>
> Many of the traditional stereotypes concerning the courage and manliness involved in the pursuit of war are psychologically questionable. As psychiatrists we know that the resort to violence is apt to stem not only from anger or feelings of strength but also from feelings of fear and inner weakness. It requires great strength and moral courage to carry on some forms of conflict without resorting to violence (1964, p. 118).

A Second Look at the Springs of Aggressive Acts

In the light of accumulating research, psychologists and social scientists have felt the necessity in recent years of examining the springs of aggressive deeds more carefully. After World War II, there was a crop of post-mortem verdicts in professional journals (including the *Journal of Abnormal and Social Psychology* published by the American Psychological Association) analyzing the horrors of the recent war in such terms as "collective guilt," "early childhood frustrations" of Axis leaders, and "unleashing of hidden aggressive tendencies" accumulated during the critical period preceding the war. Shortly thereafter, psychologists, social scientists, and psychiatrists turned to more serious study of the causes of aggressive tendencies and deeds. Necessarily, such study required considerations outside the provincialism of their particular specialty. They gave more receptive consideration to evidence from various disciplines.

They found, for example, studies of the American soldier conducted during the war (Stouffer *et al.*, 1949). Included were answers to questions about their reasons for fighting. The soldiers were the men actually doing the fighting, in situations in which the expression of aggressive feelings toward the enemy was socially permissible. Yet the majority of the soldiers said they fought to "get the job done," or because they did not want to let their outfits down. Only 2 per cent said they fought out of anger, revenge, or "fighting spirit." Another 3 per cent gave replies that might be interpreted as aggressive, such as "making a better world," "crushing the aggressor," "belief in what I am fighting for" (p. 109). Certainly aggressive and vindictive feelings were not the most salient reported by these American fighting men.

Such reports led to a closer look at the locus of aggressive and destructive emotions, since quite clearly they were not universal. Pear commented on this point, asking whether wars were the outcome of aggressive impulses of the general populace or whether such impulses had to be fanned in the name of things sacred and just to a people. He reached the following conclusion about a theory of war based on individual impulses toward aggression:

> It fails to distinguish between the aggressiveness of the warmakers, which can be very real indeed (though frequently personal greed, still socially disapproved if found out, masquerades as socially approved aggressiveness) and the attitudes of the general population, many of whom may not know of the impending war, of the combatant, the semi-combatant, and non-combatant soldiers, and of the victims. In a war involving more than half the population of the world, a vast number of people who had nothing to do with declaring war

suffered passively. Often aggressiveness had to be stirred up and intensified even in the fighters (we have recently read about the experimental army "hate school" abolished as a result of psychiatrists' reports), in the uniformed sections many people of both sexes lived an unaggressive life and yet helped to win the war, "backroom boys" and scientists are unlikely to have done their best thinking if viscerally stirred: "beating the enemy" cannot have been a constant day-and-night goal giving incentive to all non-combatants, as the excellent book *War Factory*, among others, showed (1950, pp. 40–41).

At about the same time, another eminent psychologist known for his continued interest in "personal factors" wrote on the "role of expectancy" of war in bringing about conflict. Gordon Allport of Harvard University concluded:

> The people of the world — the common people themselves — never make war. They are led into war, they fight wars, and they suffer the consequences; but they do not actually make war. Hence when we say that "wars begin in the minds of men" we can mean only that *under certain circumstances leaders can provoke and organize the people of a nation to fight.* Left alone people themselves could not make war (1950, p. 43).

Foundations and organizations have arranged several joint committees of experts to pool their findings on the causes of aggressive passions and deeds. For one of these, the sessions and comments by psychologists, psychiatrists, and social scientists of various scientific positions and ideologies were published for UNESCO with Hadley Cantril as editor (1950). (The participants were Gordon W. Allport, Gilberto Freyre, Georges Gurvitch, Max Horkheimer, Arne Naess, John Richman, Harry Stack Sullivan, and Alexander Szalai.)

Despite their differences on several points, all participants agreed on several fundamental issues. Their common statement included agreement on the following conclusion: "To the best of our knowledge, there is no evidence to indicate that wars are necessary and inevitable consequences of 'human nature' as such" (p. 17).

Neither the psychodynamicist nor the newspaper commentator who concludes that wars are inevitable because of "human nature" has provided adequate evidence for his theory. The arguments begin with the observation that men make wars, then state that men make wars because they are aggressive by nature. The proof of men's aggressive nature lies in the fact that they make wars. Nothing has been added to the first observation but words to confuse the unwary.

A Note on the Frustration-Aggression Relationship

As mentioned earlier, Freud's position before he posited the "death instinct" as the source of hostile and destructive dispositions was that aggression is the result of frustration of basic drives, especially in early childhood. This earlier formulation by Freud found its most systematic expression in a highly influential book published over a quarter of a century ago (Dollard *et al.*, 1939). It advanced the theory that all aggressive behavior (excluding only instrumental acts) was the outcome of frustration, and that frustration invariably led to aggressive tendencies.

In the face of criticism from various quarters, the formulation was subsequently qualified to indicate that every frustration does not necessarily lead to aggression. In the words of one of its principal proponents of the formulation, frustration "produces instigators to a number of different types of responses, one of which is an instigation to some form of aggression" (Miller, 1941, p. 338).

Of course, frustration suffered when activities directed toward attainment of goal objects are blocked is a state of arousal and tension with some consequences. But, in a systematic examination of the possible consequences, the following questions have to be faced:

1. (a) Is every act of aggression the outcome of frustration?
   (b) Is aggression the invariable response to frustration?
2. Within what sets of circumstances and within what framework of interpersonal and group ties is frustration conducive or *not* conducive to aggressive deeds?

In relation to the first question, Berkowitz' critical survey of research (1962) led him to conclude unequivocally that "there *are* some aggressive acts . . . . that are not necessarily instigated by frustrations" (p. 30). Among such acts, he includes a number with important consequences, such as wholesale killing and destruction initiated as policies during wartime. He also cites the interesting research by Bandura and his co-workers demonstrating that children can acquire hostile modes of behavior merely by observing the aggressive actions of an adult, even when the adult is "nurturant" to the children.

J. P. Scott (1958) cites evidence from experiments on animal behavior in his own and other laboratories that there are important causes of aggressive behavior other than frustration. "For example, we have seen that the best way to train a mouse to be highly aggressive is not to frustrate him but to give him success in fighting (p. 33) . . . . *frustration leads to aggression only in a situation where the individual has a habit of being aggressive*" (p. 35). The latter generalization was based on the behavior of goats frustrated by interference with their food supply: only the more dominant animals who were habitually aggressive toward the less dominant became more aggressive as a result.

The further question of whether frustration invariably leads to aggressive behavior in animals is answered by Scott in these words: "In short, while frustration is highly likely to produce aggression, the result may also be other kinds of behavior" (p. 34).

Himmelweit (1950) reached a similar conclusion in her survey of studies of human frustration. She listed the following responses to frustration observed in different studies of human subjects: aggression, regression (lowering the level of performance), evading the situation by leaving it or daydreaming, apathy and resignation (especially for prolonged frustration), repression or "forgetting." Frequently several of these responses were observed in the same frustrating situation.

When applied to problems of hostility and prejudice between human groups, the frustration-aggression hypothesis is an inadequate and even misleading explanation of aggressive behavior and of reaction to frustration. It is misleading because it directs investigation exclusively towards an aroused psychological state and a class of actions (aggressive). Any adequate hypothesis about human behavior must include specification of the environmental circumstances in which a psychological state occurs and in which a class of actions occurs. As applied to frustration and aggression in group relations, this means that an adequate hypothesis must include statements about the culture and organizational context of both tension arousal and behavior. The second question raised above is pertinent here.

If the frustrating experience is strictly an individual affair within the context of day-to-day interpersonal relations, how can it become the basis for prejudice, injustice, and aggressive actions that follow existing dominance-subordination arrangements in society? Why is there not more variation in the targets of hostility? It is necessary to ask whether a frustration is *individually* experienced or is seen by other members of a group as a *common frustration*. If the frustration is seen as shared, does it have any bearing on the direction of the greatest prejudice and the most hostile actions toward other groups? According to an adapted version of the frustration-aggression hypothesis, the most vehement aggressive impulses should be generated among those who share the greatest frustrations.

Is the direction of prejudice and aggressive actions primarily from the most downtrodden and deprived groups toward dominant groups who maintain their mighty position, or are these not frequently directed from the mighty and powerful *toward* the underprivileged groups, who one may assume are more frustrated? Such questions direct serious consideration to the organizational or group context of frustration and of aggressive actions. Answers to such questions are necessary before we can conclude that frustration suffered by single individuals without becoming a common concern has a major role in intergroup aggression.

In concluding his studies on aggression in animals, the zoologist Scott (1958) cautioned students of violence and peace among human groups. "It is clear," he wrote, "that human societies differ a great deal, both in their ideal codes of behavior regarding fighting and in the actual amount which goes on. In some societies fighting may be considered noble, in others normal, and in still others reprehensible" (p. 99).

It should also be clear that human societies vary a great deal in *whom* they select as proper targets of hatred and aggressive acts. Further, the context of aggression within a society is not identical to that between nations, for "the fact that an entire human society may act as a unit makes war a very different phenomenon from aggressive fighting which takes place between individuals and small groups within a society. Considered objectively warfare is primarily an attribute of populations rather than of individuals" (Scott, 1958, p. 104).

Perhaps the inadequacies of the frustration-aggression hypothesis for violence within an organizational context are most striking when it is applied to lynchings or murders. Such deeds have been attributed to frustrations or deprivations suffered by the lynchers, who frequently, though not always, have included "poor whites."

There may be a grain of truth that personal frustrations have something to do with the degree and extent of brutality by individual lynchers. But the presence or absence of lynching *as an institution*, to be engaged in without serious fear of punishment, is not adequately explained in these terms. When this brutal institution is outside the bounds of the organizational and normative orientation of the group, when it is forbidden and punishable, the mere thought of such deeds in concert with one's fellows is personally appalling, no matter what the individual's frustrations may be. The point was well made in a comparison reported by Klineberg:

> White Brazilians are, on the whole, much more economically frustrated than white Americans. The economic standards of the former are definitely much lower, and relatively many more of them live near or at a bare subsistence level. There are fluctuations in economic conditions in Brazil, just as in the United States. However, there are no lynchings of Brazilian Negroes . . . This fact makes it clearly inadequate to explain aggression against Negro or, in more general terms, hostility against other groups (which may take the form of war in extreme cases) entirely in terms of the aggressive impulses developed within the individual as a result of his frustrations (1950, p. 198).

It would be difficult to contend that there are no white Americans frustrated for reasons of poverty or lack of status. But despite this, it may be safe to predict that lynching and publicly condoned murder will be driven out-of-bounds in the United States, including the South. If so, it will be because of a changing context for intergroup behavior. This changing context will reflect the determined efforts of many Americans toward equal civil rights for all citizens.

Relationships within and between human groups, which form the context for frustration and associated aggression toward others because of their group membership, set limits for the degree and targets of aggression and chart the direction of what is desirable, or even ideal, in intergroup action. Frustration and aggression are undeniable human phenomena. Unless they are assessed within the context of group relationships, researchers can scarcely hope to have more than fragments of data, useful for valid predictions only in the restricted interpersonal relationships of the laboratory.

The next chapter will develop the implications of the study of frustration, aggressive impulse, and actions within the context of group and intergroup relations. Within this context, hypotheses are generated and experiments designed for more realistic investigations of the springs of hostility and of trust between humans in different groups.

4

Guideposts for Recasting
Research Orientation

The discussion of the rise of aggressive attitudes and deeds in the last chapter suggests the need for recasting the research orientation in this vital problem area. If research operations and results are to serve as a paradigm, instead of a caricature, research on aggression or cooperation between groups has to extract its hypotheses from the actualities of these events.

The needed research orientation must start with careful analysis of the properties of intergroup attitude and behavior. Necessarily, such analysis entails the analysis of individuals as *members* of their respective groups with reciprocal ties, expectations, and clear conceptions of the bounds of propriety-impropriety and decency-indecency. The intergroup problem is not represented by individuals in a state of isolation or by an unattached individual dealing with members of a group.

The research orientation must extract its conception of what is relevant, what is related to what and in what contexts from the actualities of intergroup relations. Such an orientation requires the researcher to set up stimulus conditions that simulate as adequately as possible the conditions in which love or hate, cooperation or rivalry arise between two or more groups in actual life. This requirement, in turn, entails devising procedures and techniques appropriate to the nature of interaction between individuals and between groups. Models of human interaction adopted merely because they are "in vogue" or "handy" are likely to mutilate the flow of interaction and produce a caricature of it.

We will now turn to problems of research specifically designed for the study of friendly or hostile attitudes and behavior. The next chapter will describe research carried out within specifiable group contexts and with firsthand information about the properties of each group. The groups themselves were produced experimentally.

First, however, let us recall the differentiating character of intergroup relations and of intergroup behavior (Chapter 1). Our research on the rise of intergroup attitudes in the next chapter follows directly from this analysis of the nature of the intergroup problem. This analysis guided the formulation of the hypotheses, the plan of the study design in successive stages of interaction among members within their groups and with out-groups, and the choice of particular procedures and techniques.

THE INTERGROUP PROBLEM

Let us start as we did in the first chapter with the obvious manifestations of intergroup relations. Groups in transaction with one another over a period of time rarely remain neutral toward one another. Between them and their individual members, there develop reciprocal states of friendship or hatred, trust or mistrust, aggressive intent or willingness to give a helping hand. This is the undeniable fact of social life.

The difficult task is to trace the course of these intergroup states from their inception. As emphasized before, the positive or negative emotions between groups are not self-generated. Underlying these states, there is frustration inflicted or satisfaction aroused, but neither is a strictly private affair of the individuals in question. Rather, the frustration or satisfaction is aroused as their groups pursue activities with particular designs, objectives, and claims on one another.

Frustration suffered by members of a group at the hands of an out-group and satisfactions experienced as a member, owing to the deeds or declarations of the out-group, are not necessarily in the same mold as those experienced in immediate interpersonal relations, as husband or wife, personal friend or rival. Nor is every state of friendship or enmity, every instance of pulling together or pulling apart among human beings a case of intergroup relations. The word "group" in the phrase "intergroup relations" is not a superfluous label. Our claim is the study of relations between groups and intergroup attitudes of their respective members. We therefore must consider both the properties of the groups themselves and the consequences of membership on individuals. Otherwise, whatever we are studying, we are not studying intergroup problems.

Membership in a group has demonstrable consequences for the individual's feeling of acceptance or rejection, of "belonging" or "not belonging," which are closely related to the properties of the group. Accordingly our first concern should be to have a clear conception of what constitutes a *group* and of the effects of membership in groups. A definition of the concept improvised merely for research convenience will not carry us far if we are interested in the *validity* of our conclusions.

The task of specifying group properties can be carried out only through an *interdisciplinary approach*. Not all problems pertaining to groups and their relations are psychological. Groups and their relations are studied on appropriate *levels of analysis* by men in different social sciences. From the extensive literature on in-group and intergroup relations, we extracted crucial leads for a realistic conception of groups and their relations (Sherif and Sherif, 1953).

Abstracting the minimum essential properties characterizing actual groups, we attained a definition of groups of any description (Chapter 1). The definition bears repeating here: a *group* is a social unit that consists of a number of individuals (1) who, at a given time, stand in status and role relationships with one another, stabilized in some degree, and (2) who possess, explicitly or implicitly, a set of norms or values regulating the behavior of individual members, at least in matters of consequence to the group.

Intergroup relations refer to relations between groups thus defined. Intergroup attitude (such as prejudice) and intergroup behavior (such as discriminatory practice) refer to the attitude revealed and the behavior manifested by members of groups collectively or individually. The distinguishing characteristic of an intergroup attitude or behavior is its relationship to membership in a social unit. This relationship has to be made explicit in research on these problems.

Unrepresentative intergroup attitude and behavior are certainly important psychological facts. But they are not what makes the study of intergroup relations so crucial in human affairs. The problem of intergroup relations is not primarily the problem of *deviate behavior* by a few individuals.

The bounds for the attitudes of members in different groups toward one another are set by the nature of functional relations between groups. Groups may be competing to attain some goal or vital prize, in which the success of one group necessarily means the failure of the other. One group may have claims on another group to manage, control, or exploit them, to take over their actual or assumed rights and possessions. On the other hand, groups may have complementary goals, so that each may attain its goal without hindrance from the others or even with their helping hand.

Although relations between groups are the limiting determinant, various other factors have to be included for an adequate account of the resultant intergroup trends and products (such as norms for positive or negative treatments, stereotypes of own and other groups, and so on). Among these factors are the kind of leadership, the degree of solidarity, and the kind of norms that prevail within each, especially those regulating social distance. Reciprocal intergroup appraisal of relative strengths and resources, and the intellectual level each has attained in assessing its own worth and rights in relation to other groups need special mention among these factors. Frustration, deprivation, and gratification in the life histories of the individual members also have to be considered for a rounded account.

Theories of intergroup relations positing one sovereign factor (such as type of leadership, national character, individual frustrations) have, at best, explained some selectively chosen cases. Of course, leadership counts and the prevailing social distance scale counts in shaping intergroup attitude and behavior. So do structure and practices within each group, and so do the personal frustrations of individual members. But none of them completely determines the particular trend of intergroup behavior at a given time. They all contribute, but none determines the trends of intergroup behavior singly. Intergroup behavior can be explained only in terms of the entire frame of reference in which all these various factors operate in an interdependent way.

The relative weights of the various factors in determining intergroup trends and practices are not fixed. Their importance varies according to the particular set of conditions prevailing at the time. For example, in cases of more or less closed, highly organized, and homogeneous groups and at times of greater stability, the prevailing social distance scale and traditional practices toward out-groups have great weight in determining the intergroup behavior of individual members. When groups become more interdependent and during times of transition or change, other factors will contribute more heavily. In these latter cases, a greater discrepancy will be found between expressed attitude and actual intergroup behavior in various situations, as has been insistently pointed out by some leading investigators in this area. Alliances and combinations among groups that seem strange bedfellows are not infrequent in the present world of flux and tension.

THEORY AND RESEARCH ON INTERGROUP ATTITUDE AND BEHAVIOR

Because of their importance in social psychology, two other approaches to intergroup behavior deserve special mention. A recapitulation of these approaches will help to clarify the distinctive features of the experiments to be reported in the next chapter.

One of these approaches, as we have seen, considers the individual's personal history of frustration as the main cause of aggressiveness. Certainly aggression is *one* of the possible consequences of frustration experienced by the individual. But, for individual frustration to have an appreciable effect on the course of *intergroup* trends and to be a causal factor in standardization of a negative out-group attitude or stereotype, it has to be shared by other group members and come to the foreground *as an issue* in in-group and intergroup interaction. The realistic contribution of frustration as a factor can be studied only when taken in the framework of in-group and intergroup relations.

The second approach concentrates primarily on group processes *within* the group. It is assumed that measures introduced to increase responsibility, cooperativeness, and harmony within the group will be conducive to bringing about cooperativeness and harmony between groups. This assumption amounts to extrapolating the properties of in-group relations to intergroup relations. Probably, when friendly attitudes and relations already prevail between groups, cooperative and harmonious in-group relations may contribute to solutions of mutual problems that arise between them. However, there are numerous cases in which in-group cooperativeness and harmony contribute effectively to intergroup competitiveness and conflict.

The important generalization to be drawn from this discussion is that attitude and behavior toward members of out-groups cannot be merely extrapolated from knowledge about (1) personal experiences, apart from the individual's membership in his group, or (2) the properties of interaction among members *within* his group. The limiting factor bounding his attitude and behavior toward out-groups is the nature of relationships *between* the groups.

The area of interaction between groups does not consist of a vacuum, or the cozy atmosphere of a conference room. The character of interaction between groups is not determined only by the character of relations and norms prevailing *within* each of the groups. The area of interaction between groups, whether full of tension or freely flowing cooperation, may produce reverberations within each of the groups in question.

Groups have interests that may overlap or conflict with the interests of other groups. These overlapping or conflicting interests are frequently of common concern to members of the respective groups. They may relate to values or goals shared by the members. They may involve a real or imagined threat to their mutual safety, an economic interest, a political advantage, a military consideration, prestige, or any one of many other important issues.

Unless practices and norms within the group become an *issue* in relations between groups, they are not readily transferred from the realm of the membership into the area of interaction between groups. As numerous cases from the colonial period eloquently testify, democracy within a nation need not be transferred to dealings with other groups outside.

The course of intergroup relations and their change are greatly influenced by the issues between the groups. However, once a particular issue comes to the foreground in their encounters, it may become the dominant anchorage for interaction between the groups in other matters as well.

Inconsistencies in Intragroup and Intergroup Behavior

If the preceding analysis is correct, one is perfectly justified in asking why, on occasion, we find striking inconsistencies in behavior related to group and intergroup issues. Anyone familiar with colonial practices, or with those of any unit claiming hegemony with a big-brother status over others can tell us that there are many inconsistencies in attitude and behavior with the change from an in-group to an intergroup context.

For example, hostility toward other groups is, in some cases, proportional to the solidarity and loyalty of members within their groups. Efforts to attain supremacy over the out-group may be pursued simultaneously with declarations of the equality of man.

Such cases appear inconsistent only when they are not assessed within the framework of their respective group or intergroup system. Within the appropriate framework, the apparently inconsistent attitude and action become accountable, though not necessarily justifiable.

Inconsistencies in attitude and action are not peculiar to groups in encounters with others outside of their national boundaries. Within a society, an individual may be an identified member of various groupings. As a result, his behavior may appear highly inconsistent or contradictory in different situations. An illustration is the case of some union members who actively participated in the Detroit race riots (Lee and Humphrey, 1943). The union taught and practiced nonsegregation. If these union members had been nothing but good union members, they would not have participated in the riots. But they were also members of families, neighborhood groups, churches, and ethnic groups and, as they were reminded in many ways from childhood on, they were "white." Long before they became members of the union, these groups were major reference groups for them. It is hardly surprising that in a situation in which they had to choose between being a "regular person" in their major reference groups and acting as a good union member, many of them acted contrary to the union's teachings, perhaps with no thought of doing otherwise.

To be sure, the behavior of individuals may be inconsistent for a number of reasons, including idiosyncratic ones related to continual thwarting of basic motives or persistent conflicts in interpersonal situations. The point here is that many of the inconsistencies in behavior related to intergroup problems fall into an orderly and coherent pattern when analyzed within the framework of the individual's various reference groups and their salience to him in different situations.

When all aspects of a society — from its grass-roots communities, churches, and schools to its mass media and officialdom — agree in word and deed upon the "place" and the characteristics of a group, the individual whose own attitude toward that group diverges is a notable exception. He may be so far out of bounds as to incur severe penalties or corrective attempts. He is the deviant or the noncomformist *par excellence.*

In a rapidly changing world, many instances can be cited of men and women with loyalties and vital personal interests in several different groupings with contradictory directions and goals. In such cases, the question of the salience to the individual of the various group references becomes significant. Williams (1964) has documented numerous instances of apparent inconsistencies in how a person says he feels, what he says he will do with reference to treatment of Negroes, and what he actually does in a specific situation. Surveys in Washington, D.C., and several border states prior to official desegregation attempts revealed the majority opposed to desegregation, yet in many such localities desegregation was accomplished without protest or violence.

These "inconsistencies" reflect the fact that individuals are likely to respond to specific situations in terms of the reference group most salient to them or most pertinent in the situation. Thus, a person who is both against desegregation and strongly loyal to a government by law can speak his opinion to an interviewer, but his loyalty to the government prevents active obstructionism or violence against a desegregation law. A businessman who believes in race superiority doctrines may desegregate his business establishment along with other businesses because it becomes necessary for the common business interest (cf. Jones and Long, 1965).

The voting behavior of United States senators and congressmen is sometimes puzzling to a person looking for consistency of belief and action. In a number of cases, persons who otherwise have records which seem consistently "liberal" or "conservative" cast votes that are "surprising," that is, are inconsistent with the rest of their records. This has occurred on foreign policy matters and on civil rights legislation in particular.

The "surprises" turn out to be not surprising at all when viewed within the context of the legislator's group reference. Those familiar with the dominant interests and prevailing attitudes of the region or state the legislator represents realize that most frequently the "surprising" vote is the only alternative open to a man who strongly identifies his future with serving in the legislative halls and faces sure termination of his political career if he votes contrary to clear-cut positions taken by the most powerful or the majority of his constituents (cf. *Time*, January 22, 1965, pp. 14–18).

Recently a study of attitude and behavior that appeared quite contradictory, even fickle, was made by E. Q. Campbell and T. F. Pettigrew (1959a, 1959b). Following the violence accompanying the initial attempt to desegregate public high schools in Little Rock, Arkansas, in 1957, forty-two ministers were interviewed in that city. Of these, thirteen were avowed segregationists, eight were active integrationists throughout, and five were opposed to violence and offered neutral prayers during the period but were classified as tacit segregationists on the basis of the interviews. The remainder, including almost all the ministers of high prestige in the community, favored desegregation but were inactive after initial protests at the start of the crisis and "peace prayer services."

As men of God, all those who interpreted their commitment as bearing the message of peace, justice, and equality would have been consistent in voicing this message to their congregations and to the public. Only the eight "active" integrationists chose this course. Most of them were younger men who had headed small churches for only a short time before the crisis. Within a year, one had concluded that he could no longer communicate with his congregation and requested a transfer, and several others were removed from their pulpits.

The dilemma for the Little Rock minister centered around the fact that his congregation was largely opposed to desegregation. The most support that any of the integrationist ministers estimated in their congregations was 40 per cent, and the average estimate of those opposing desegregation was 75 per cent. Although the ministers also thought of themselves as men of God and as members of a larger church, church officials offered little support for the Protestant minister who took the risk of splitting or alienating his congregation. In order to maintain membership, keep up the finances and facilities of the church, and avoid disrupting "Christian fellowship," the majority of the ministers simply did nothing. In contrast to their definition by the avowed segregationist ministers as a bunch of "race mixers," these inactive ministers came to feel courageous merely for keeping quiet or daring to give a sermon on brotherly love without reference to the race issue.

Campbell and Pettigrew make the conflict very clear:

> Defense of racial integration in Little Rock came to mean lost members, lost financial support, and a lost opportunity to build the proposed north wing. And these results were concrete evidence of a minister not performing his "proper" duties. . . . Church superiors, rather than protecting such men, keep a close eye on administrative records and usually act accordingly. . . . Given this denominational structure, it was infinitely easier for the clergyman to continue on as the quiet and coordinating "shepherd of his flock" than to enter the conflict. If he remained silent, he received appreciation from his congregation for not being like the ministers "who dragged their churches into the whole mess," and he did not have to

face the unaccustomed abuse from the community (1959b, pp. 130, 131).

In time of change, individuals often are caught between the role expectations of the traditional community and the demands of developing trends that require its re-orientation toward enlarged loyalties and identifications of individuals. As the older framework is criss-crossed by developing trends that require giving up old prejudices and narrow alignments, individuals caught between them are bound to exhibit inconsistencies as one or the other loyalty becomes salient from one situation to the next.

The inevitable conclusion is that such inconsistencies between attitude and behavior become accountable when considered within their appropriate framework: interpersonal, within group, or between group and group. We repeat that logical accounting does not make such cases justifiable. It merely finds order and coherence where none seemed to exist. Specifying the appropriate framework of the behavior makes it possible to avoid the hackneyed accusation that people who behave inconsistently in these matters are merely freakish or volatile by nature.

GENERAL FORMULATION OF INTERGROUP PROBLEMS

Guided by the considerations presented in this chapter, a program of research was initiated in 1948 to study the rise of positive and negative intergroup attitude and behavior in their appropriate framework. There was serious concern over the correspondence between the conception of the studies and the actualities of intergroup relations that the studies purported to investigate. The hypotheses were formulated on the basis of extensive surveys of literature on the rise of friendly and hostile attitudes and engagements between groups in racial, industrial, and political areas. The specific hypotheses tested were derived from a generalization extracted from these surveys. The generalization may be stated briefly as follows:

When a group forms, one of the products is a delineation of "we" from "they" — the "we" including the members of the group. The "we" thus delineated comes, in time, to embody a host of qualities and values to be upheld, defended, and cherished. Offenses from without or deviations from within are reacted to with corrective, defensive, and, at times, offensive measures.

A set of qualities, traits, or stereotypes are attributed to other groups which comprise the "they" from the point of view of the in-group. The characteristics attributed to other groups are not a direct outgrowth of in-group practices or norms, but are not entirely independent of them. Their nature depends upon the actual or perceived relations between the groups in question. (In some cases, interested parties within or outside the group may succeed in presenting a picture of relationships between the groups with their own special interests in mind.) The traits attributed to the out-group may be favorable, unfavorable, or both, depending upon the relationships group members perceive between the two groups.

The relationships between the groups following successive intergroup encounters are limited by the interests and goals of the respective groups. If the interests and directions of the groups are integrated or harmonious, the "they" group is pictured in a positive or favorable light. But if the activities and goals of the interacting groups clash, then the characteristics attributed to the out-group are invariably negative and derogatory.

One group may take the position that the other is in its way, interfering with its goals and vital interests. One group may even insist that the other should be working in its interests. One group may have goals that cannot be attained without loss by the other group. In these cases, stereotyped characteristics and beliefs about the out-group develop, their prime logic being justification of the "we" group's position. (As noted in Chapter 2, race superiority doctrines are justifications of this kind.)

From this overall generalization about the rise of positive or negative intergroup attitudes, specific hypotheses were derived about the formation of groups, about in-group attitudes and expectations, and about the rise of hostile intergroup actions and attitudes. Hypotheses on the rise of hostile intergroup attitudes served, in turn, as premises for specific predictions about changes from negative relations toward friendly and cooperative transactions, with correspondingly favorable images of the out-group.

5

The Experiments

Hypotheses to be tested experimentally were derived from the orientation stated in Chapter 4. The orientation required a study design with a definite sequence of stages, each designed to establish experimental conditions for hypotheses whose testing also depended upon the outcome of the previous stage. The sequence can be described briefly.

For experimental purposes it was important to start from scratch with individuals who had no previous relationships with one another. The individuals were chosen very carefully, as we shall see, to rule out explanations of the results other than those being tested.

In order to test our formulation of the essential characteristics of intergroup relations, the next step was to produce distinct groups, each with a definite organization (leader and followers) and a set of norms for behavior. To insure control over conditions in which groups formed and came into contact, the experiments were conducted in isolated camp sites completely at the disposal of the research program.

Groups were formed. The natural history of their formation was traced step by step. Then for the first time the groups were brought into functional contact. They were brought into contact initially under conditions designed to produce competition, hostility, and social distances between them. Later, they met under conditions designed to test hypotheses about the reduction of hostility and derogatory stereotypes.

Three separate experiments were conducted, each lasting approximately three weeks, in different locations and with different subjects (cf. Sherif, 1951; Sherif and Sherif, 1953; Sherif, White, and Harvey, 1955; Sherif *et al.*, 1961). A composite picture of the conduct and findings of the three studies will be presented here, with specification of the source when this is feasible without confusing the account. The first experiment, conducted in 1949 in Connecticut, was carried through the stage of intergroup conflict. All the hypotheses presented here were formulated before the second study, but the systematic sequence of stages in that study had to be terminated after the rise of intergroup hostility. The third experiment, conducted at Robbers Cave, Oklahoma, was carried through the sequence of group formation, intergroup conflict, and reduction of intergroup conflict which was contingent upon cooperative activities between erstwhile hostile groups.

Choice of Subjects

Because the experiments were performed at camp sites, subjects were selected who would find camping a natural and fascinating activity: boys between eleven and twelve years old. In order to eliminate, as much as possible, alternative explanations for events that transpired in the experiments, the selection procedures were long and careful. Interviews were held with each boy's teachers, school officials, and family. School and medical records were studied, and scores were obtained on psychological tests. Each boy was observed in natural give-and-take with agemates in the classroom and during athletic and informal interpersonal activities.

As a result of the methods of selecting subjects, the results could not be explained in any of the following alternative ways:

1. Previous acquaintance or personal ties among the boys. Boys were chosen from different schools and neighborhoods to eliminate this possibility.

2. Neurotic tendencies, undue instability, or excessively frustrating situations in past history. The boys were healthy, well adjusted in school and neighborhood, members of stable families with both parents living at home (no broken homes), and with no record of past disturbances in behavior. Members of minority

groups who might have suffered from social discrimination were not included.

3. Pronounced differences in background or phsyical appearance. All subjects were selected from stable, white Protestant families from the middle socioeconomic level. While they displayed the normal range of individual differences, these were equalized during the stage of group formation by matching boys in the different groups as much as possible according to size and skills.

Research Procedures and the Validity Problem

As in any experiment, the chief claim to validity must lie in the correspondence between the research conditions and the actualities the experiment purports to study. Our concern with validity led to the particular sequence of the study just described. It also dictated the major features of the research procedures and methods for data collection.

The experimental conditions for each successive stage were defined in terms of the *properties* of problem situations the subjects faced. All problem situations were introduced in a naturalistic setting, in keeping with activities usually carried out in such settings. All problem situations were selected to be highly appealing, on the basis of prior study of the subjects' interests. Through manipulation of objects, facilities, and timing, it was possible to introduce the procedures with a minimum of verbal instruction and without the individuals being aware that each step was planned to study intergroup relations experimentally. The experimental nature of the study required that the problem situations at each stage meet the criteria specified for conditions of that stage. Beyond this, every effort was made so that the activities and the flow of interpersonal interaction as they occurred were as natural as possible.

Since the knowledge that one is a "research subject" and is being observed constantly has definite effects on behavior, the subjects were not aware that data were being collected or that the sequence of events was experimentally planned. All research staff appeared in the roles of personnel in a usual camp situation: senior counselors (observers), camp director, handyman, and so on. In these capacities, they observed the boys throughout their waking hours, recording symbols and other notes only when out of the subjects' sight and expanding them into a report later each day.

The validity of the findings was cross-checked by using a *combination of data-gathering methods* at every step. In addition to reports of observation on interaction and ratings made by "senior counselors," independent ratings were made by observers not familiar with the groups in situations in which the group was engaged in lively interaction. Sociometric choices were obtained from the subjects themselves in interviews that appeared to them as casual conversations. At choice points, laboratory-like techniques were introduced to assess their attitudes through judgment tasks presented to them as games.

In summarizing the research, we rely on recurrent observations that were checked by one or more of these techniques.

STAGE OF SPONTANEOUS INTERPERSONAL FRIENDSHIP CHOICES

HYPOTHESES

A. When unacquainted individuals with similar backgrounds meet in interaction situations of common appeal to them, interpersonal friendship clusters will develop on the basis of personal attractions, common interests, and affinities.

B. These spontaneous friendship ties will be reversed in favor of fellow group members when friends participate separately in the formation of different groups.

The primary purpose of this stage was to reduce the possibility that groups formed in the experiment proper would be based initially on sheer personal attraction. When the boys arrived at the site, they were all housed in one large bunkhouse. All activities were camp-wide, with free choice of buddies, eating companions, and the like.

After the boys had begun to be consistent in associating with one or two others in various activities, each was asked informally who his best friends were (sociometric choices). Then the boys were divided into two different cabins, so that about two-thirds of their best friends were in the other cabin. (The pain of separation was eased by allowing each cabin to go at once on an overnight hike and camp-out, something all had wanted to do.) Following the stage of group formation, they were again asked who their best friends were, specifying that they could choose from the entire camp.

Table 1 gives the data from the 1949 study showing how friendship choices based on personal attraction were reversed after groups had actually formed. These procedures were replicated in 1953 with almost identical results.

Table 1

Reversal of Friendship Choices Before and After Group Formation

Persons Chosen In:	Persons Choosing From:					
	Group A			Group B		
	Before	After	Difference	Before	After	Difference
	%	%	%	%	%	%
Group A	35.1	95.0	59.9	65.0	12.3	−52.7
Group B	64.9	5.0	−59.9	35.0	87.7	52.7

CONCLUSIONS AND IMPLICATIONS

From the results in this stage, we conclude that interaction in pleasant activities among similar individuals is conducive to formation of small friendship clusters based on personal attraction and common interests. By separating the friendship clusters before the stage of group formation, the possibility of explaining group formation primarily on that basis is eliminated. Further, the findings show that choice of friends is affected by the formation of groups, more than half of the choices shifting away from strictly personal preferences toward friendship within their own group.

These findings may tell us something about the choice of friends and personal associates in daily life. The popular notions that, "I choose friends because of my own personal preferences" or that "We all should be free to choose our friends" are misleading, particularly when used to justify exclusionist practices by organized groups (cf. Lee, 1955). As the results show, friendship choices shift readily from strictly interpersonal attractions toward in-group exclusiveness, as a part of group formation and functioning. Freedom to choose friends on the basis of personal preferences within an organization turns out to be freedom to choose among persons selected according to the rules of membership established by the organization.

STAGE OF GROUP FORMATION

HYPOTHESES

1. When a number of individuals without previously established relationships interact in conditions that embody goals with common appeal value to the individuals and that require interdependent activities for their attainment, a definite group structure consisting of differentiated status positions and roles will be produced.

1a. Appraisals of performance by group members will vary with the status of the member being judged, status being defined as *effective initiative* in group interaction. The higher an individual's status the greater will be the tendency to overestimate his performance.

2. When individuals interact under the conditions stated in Hypothesis 1, norms regulating their behavior in relations with one another and in activities commonly engaged in will become standardized, concomitant with the rise of group structure.

This stage of the experiment started by dividing the subjects into two bunches, matched as closely as possible in terms of size and skills of the individuals composing them. In the 1954 experiment at Robbers Cave, this stage was the first, since the previous experiments had eliminated explanation of friendship choices on the basis of strictly personal preference. The boys arrived on two separate buses and settled in cabins at a considerable distance. Thus, belonging to their cabin seemed entirely natural. Contact between the two groups was prevented until the next stage.

In this stage, the boys engaged in many activities, but all were in harmony with specifications for group formation. All required interdependent activities among the boys in a cabin to reach a common goal as specified in the hypotheses. They included camping out, cooking, improving swimming places, transporting canoes over rough terrain to the water, and various games.

As they faced problem situations, played, and worked together, the boys in each unit pooled their efforts, organized duties, and divided up tasks of work and play. Different individuals assumed different responsibilities. One excelled in cooking. Another led in athletics. Others, though not outstanding in any particular skill, could be counted on to pitch in and do their level best in anything the group attempted. One or two boys seemed to disrupt activities, to start teasing at the wrong moment or offer useless suggestions. A few boys consistently had good suggestions and showed ability to coordinate the efforts of others in carrying them through. Within a few days, one person had proved himself more resourceful in the latter respect than the others. Thus, rather quickly, a leader and lieutenants emerged. Some boys sifted toward the bottom of the heap, while others jockeyed for higher positions of respect.

This process of group formation may be illustrated during a cookout in the woods. The staff supplied the boys with unprepared food. When they got hungry, one boy started to build a fire, asking for help in getting wood. Another attacked the raw hamburger to make patties. Others prepared a place to put buns, relishes, and the like. Two mixed soft drinks from flavoring and sugar. One boy who stood around without helping was told by others to "get to it." Shortly the fire was blazing and the cook had hamburgers sizzling. Two boys distributed them as rapidly as they became browned. Soon it was time for the watermelon. A low-ranking member took a knife and started toward the melon. Some of the others protested. The most highly regarded boy in the group took the knife, saying, "You guys who yell the loudest get yours last."

The relative positions in the group were rated by observers and independent raters primarily on the basis of their *effective initiative* in the group. These ratings were also checked by informal sounding of the boys' opinions as to who got things started, who got things done, and who could be counted on to support group activities (see Figure 1). When these measurements by observers and sociometric choice checked, we could conclude that a group organization had formed, as predicted in the hypotheses.

In the 1953 experiment, we obtained data for Hypothesis 1a on the status relations in each group through a game requiring each boy to evaluate the performance of his fellow members. Before an important baseball game, a target board was set up, with the pretense of making practice in pitching more interesting. There were no marks on the front of the board for the boys to judge objectively how close the ball came to a bull's-eye, but, unknown to them, the board was wired to flashing lights behind so that an observer could see exactly where the ball hit. The result was that the boys consistently overestimated the performance of the most highly regarded members of their group and tended to underestimate the scores of low-ranking members. In other words,

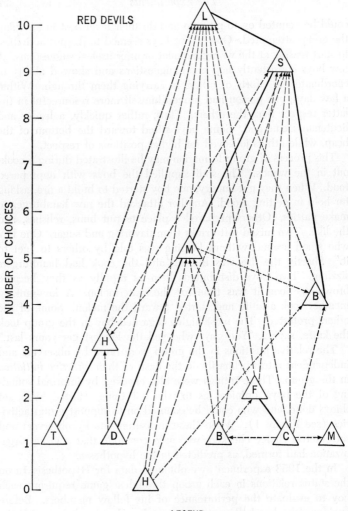

RED DEVILS

NUMBER OF CHOICES

LEGEND
—— RECIPROCATED CHOICES
- - - -> ONE-WAY CHOICES

Figure 5.1a

Status structure of the Red Devils.

BULL DOGS

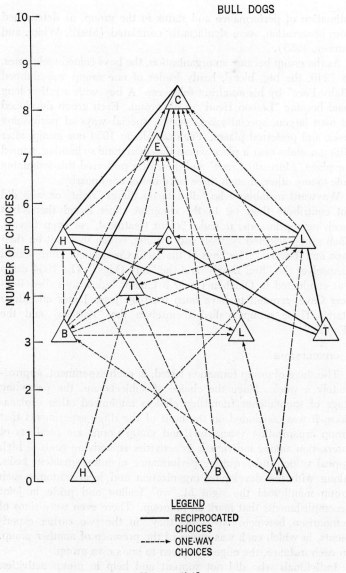

LEGEND

—— RECIPROCATED
CHOICES

----→ ONE-WAY
CHOICES

Figure 5.1b

Status structure of the Bull Dogs.

estimation of performance and status in the group, as determined
from observation, were significantly correlated (Sherif, White, and
Harvey, 1955).

As the group became an organization, the boys coined nicknames.
In 1949, the big, blond, hardy leader of one group was dubbed
"Baby Face" by his admiring followers. A boy with a rather long
head became "Lemon Head" to his group. Each group developed
its own jargon, special jokes, secrets, special ways of performing
tasks, and preferred places. For example, in 1954 one group, after
killing a snake near a place where they had gone swimming, named
the place "Moccasin Creek" and thereafter preferred this swimming
hole to any other, though there were better ones nearby.

Wayward members who failed to do things "right" or who did
not contribute their bit to the common effort found themselves
receiving reprimands, ridicule, "silent treatment," or even threats.
Each group selected symbols and a name, which they put on their
caps and T-shirts. The boys in the 1949 Connecticut study called
themselves the "Red Devils" and the "Bull Dogs." The 1954 camp
was conducted in Oklahoma near a famous hideaway called Robbers Cave, reputed to have been used by Jesse James and Belle
Starr. These groups called themselves the "Rattlers" and the
"Eagles."

CONCLUSIONS

The stage of group formation lasted, in each experiment, approximately a week. Since the choice of subjects and the preceding
stage of spontaneous friendship choices minimized other explanations, it was concluded on the basis of the three experiments that
group organization (structure) and group norms are products of
interaction among individuals in activities embodying goals of high
appeal value, and requiring performance of interdependent tasks.
Along with the developing organization and local customs, each
group manifested the signs of "we" feeling and pride in joint
accomplishments that mark an in-group. There even were signs of
comparison between "we" and "they" in the two earlier experiments, in which each was aware of the presence of another group.
In each instance, the edge was given to one's own group.

Individuals who did not support and help in group activities,
who tried to "bully" others, or who actively interfered with
projects in progress were subjected to correctives and cold-shoulder-
ing by others. By the end of the stage, however, most behavior in
the group was in accord with the customary *modus operandi* that

had been established, with very little need for frequent correctives. The Bull Dogs, at the initiative of their leader, instituted a standard penalty for getting "out of line" (removing a given number of stones from their swimming hole), which was administered by the leader with the consent of the entire membership.

Though isolated from currents of ordinary life, the groups that formed inevitably reflected the general culture and the surrounds of which they were parts. The names chosen for the groups are one example; nicknames, preferences in activities, the development of democratic procedures, and the interest in competitive games are others. Even these little experimental groups reflected a cultural framework and, as the next stage showed, no group structure had a wall impenetrable from the outside.

STAGE OF INTERGROUP CONFLICT

HYPOTHESES

1. When members of two groups come into contact with one another in a series of activities that embody goals which each urgently desires, but which can be attained by one group only at the expense of the other, competitive activity toward the goal changes, over time, into hostility between the groups and their members.

2. In the course of such competitive interaction toward a goal available only to one group, unfavorable attitudes and images (stereotypes) of the out-group come into use and are standardized, placing the out-group at a definite social distance from the in-group.

3. Conflict between two groups tends to produce an increase in solidarity *within* the groups.

4. The heightened solidarity and pride in the group will be reflected in overestimation of the achievements by fellow group members and lower estimates of the achievements by members of the out-group.

5. Relations between groups that are of consequence to the groups in question, including conflict, tend to produce changes in the organization and practices *within* the groups.

The rise of persistent conflict between groups and hostile attitudes toward each other were predicted even though each group was composed of normal, well-adjusted individuals, and even though there were no differences between the groups in terms of sociocultural background or marked physical characteristics.

In order that contact between the groups could be specified, the groups had no encounters as groups prior to this stage. (Indeed, in 1954 the two groups were not even aware of each other's presence until just before this stage.)

Because these were American boys, who are keenly interested in competitive sports, the necessary experimental conditions were easily created. As though acceding to the boys' requests, the staff arranged a tournament of games: baseball, touch football, tug of war, a treasure hunt and so on, with prizes for the winning group.

The tournament started in a spirit of good sportsmanship, but as it progressed good feeling began to evaporate. The "good sportsmanship" cheer customarily given after a game, "2-4-6-8-who do we appreciate," followed by the name of the other group, turned into "2-4-6-8 who do we appreci-*hate*." Soon members of each group began to call their rivals "stinkers," "sneaks," and "cheats." The boys in the 1949 camp turned against buddies whom they had chosen as "best friends" when they first arrived. The rival groups made threatening posters and planned raids, collecting secret hoards of green apples as ammunition.

In the Robbers Cave study, the Eagles, after defeat in a game, burned a banner left behind by the Rattlers. The next morning the Rattlers seized the Eagles' flag when they arrived on the athletic field. From that time on, name-calling, scuffling, and raids were the rule of the day. A large proportion of the boys in each group gave negative ratings to the character of *all* boys in the other. When the tournament was over, they refused to have anything more to do with members of the other group.

However, another effect of intergroup conflict was to increase solidarity, cooperativeness, and morale *within* each group. It is noteworthy that the heightening of cooperativeness and democratic interaction *within* each group did *not* carry over to a group's treatment of the other group.

Near the end of this stage, the members of each group found the other group and its members so distasteful that they expressed strong preferences to have no further contact with them at all. In fact, they were subsequently reluctant even to be in pleasant situations (eating, movies, entertainments), if they knew the other group would also be in the vicinity.

At this point in 1954, a game of bean toss was introduced, with a cash prize, the aim being to see which group could collect the largest number of beans scattered on the ground within a limited time. Each person collected beans in a sack with a restricted opening, so that he could not check the number of beans in it. Through an opaque projector, the beans purportedly collected by each individual were shown briefly, and everyone wrote down his estimate of the number. Actually, thirty-five beans were exposed each time, a number sufficiently large that it could not be counted in the time available. The findings showed that members of each group, on the average, *over*estimated the number of beans collected by fellow members, and made much lower estimates of the detested out-group's performance. The tendency to *over*estimate was much greater for the group that had won the tournament of games just concluded. The losers *over*estimated their own performance and *under*estimated that of their rivals on this task.

The course of conflict between the groups did produce changes in the status and role relationships *within* groups as predicted. In one group, leadership actually changed hands when the leader who had emerged during group formation proved reluctant to take front-line action in the conflict. In another, a "bully" who had been castigated during the peaceful days of group formation, and had been rather low in status, emerged as a hero during encounters with the out-group. Practices established within the group, including techniques for team play and for executing the tug of war, were altered during the intergroup encounters. During a tug of war, one group adopted the strategy of its opponents. A great deal of time and energy within each group went into making plans and strategies to outwit and defeat the out-group, which now appeared as an "enemy."

Perhaps the net effect of intergroup conflict upon the in-groups can be illustrated best by a test situation near the end of this stage. In the 1954 study, the groups were taken to the beach at a nearby lake for an outing on a day when the beach was crowded with visitors and afforded many distractions. Despite the sheer effort needed not to get "lost in the crowd," each group stuck together, entirely absorbed in its own activities. Watching carefully for diversions of attention, the observers could find only such incidents as a boy bumping into a stranger and murmuring "Pardon me," as he rushed to join his fellows. Psychologically, other people did not "count" as far as the boys were concerned. Such intensive concentration of interests and activities within the group would have been impossible in this situation had not the groups attained a high degree of solidarity.

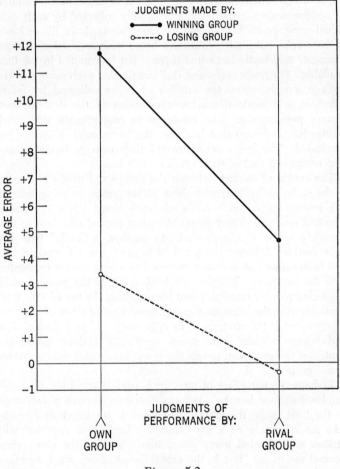

Figure 5.2

Errors in estimating a performance by victors and defeated group in intergroup tournament.

This instance of in-group solidarity and cooperativeness was observed at the very time when intergroup conflict was at its peak, during the period when the groups asserted emphatically that they would have nothing more to do with one another.

There can be no doubt that cultural and observable physical differences between groups facilitate discriminatory reactions toward members of an out-group. There can be no doubt that such differences play a part in intergroup hostility and prejudice. Yet this stage of intergroup conflict has shown that neither cultural, physical, nor economic differences are *necessary* for the rise of intergroup conflict, hostile attitudes, and stereotyped images of out-groups. Nor are maladjusted, neurotic, or unstable tendencies necessary conditions for the appearance of intergroup prejudice and stereotypes.

The *sufficient condition* for the rise of hostile and aggressive deeds (including raids on each other's cabins with destruction of property) and for the standardization of social distance justified by derogatory images of the out-group was the existence of two groups competing for goals that only one group could attain, to the dismay and frustration of the other group.

During the course of rising intergroup hostility, solidarity and cooperativeness within each group did increase. There was no indication of any transfer of these modes of behavior to the out-group. The intergroup conflict did produce changes in the patterns of relationships within each group and in the issues and practices of concern to the members of each. The sequence of events did affect the judgment of the members in their appraisals of their own and the out-group's performance.

If an outside observer had entered the situation at this point, with no information about preceding events, he could only have concluded on the basis of their behavior that these boys (who were the "cream of the crop" in their communities) were wicked, disturbed, and vicious bunches of youngsters.

STAGE OF INTERGROUP COOPERATION: REDUCTION OF INTERGROUP CONFLICT

How can two groups in conflict, each with hostile atittudes and negative images of the other and each desiring to keep the members of the detested out-group at a safe distance, be brought into cooperative interaction and friendly intercourse? When the 1954 study was done, we were not aware that this had ever been accomplished through controlled conditions that were specified in advance.

We were aware, however, of various proposals that for one reason or another were insufficient or inadequate to reduce conflict once it had heightened, to bring conflicting groups into cooperative interaction, or to reduce hostile attitudes and images.

Perhaps the most persistent concept about reducing intergroup hostility is that groups should have "accurate" (hence favorable) *information* about each other. There can be no quarrel with this proposal. Indeed, groups must know something about each other before there is any possibility of changing hostile relationships. However, all the available evidence shows that "information" is subordinate to the existing state of relationships between groups, and actually succeeds in changing this state only when it contains definite evidence of a shift in their relative power (as with the advent of Sputnik). Otherwise, the available research indicates that favorable information about the adversary is ignored, is reinterpreted to fit one's own designs, or is otherwise ineffective as the sole means of reducing intergroup conflict.

As for the related notion that information couched in appeals to moral values is sufficient in itself, the experiments contain numerous examples to the contrary. Religious services, held on Sunday (as is customary in camps of Protestant boys) with their enthusiastic support, were conducted by the same minister for each group. At our request, the topics were brotherly love, forgiveness of enemies, and cooperation. The boys arranged the services except for the sermon, to which the response was uniformly enthusiastic. Upon solemnly departing from the beautiful outdoor setting of Sunday ceremony, they returned within minutes to their concerns in defeating the detested out-group, or avoiding it, as the case might be at the time.

In the 1949 experiment, we found that the introduction of a *common enemy* in the form of another competing group was at least temporarily effective. But for two reasons, this expedient measure was not attempted again. First, the uniting of hostile groups to defeat another group is, after all, a widening of intergroup conflict on a larger scale. If pursued to its logical limits, the end result is simply a repetition of the stage of intergroup conflict with larger, hence potentially more deadly flare-ups. Second, history is replete with examples of conflicting groups who close ranks to face an enemy and then resume the same old conflicts when the enemy is vanquished.

Both on a community, regional, and international scale, *conferences of leaders* are frequently held and proposed as the means to settle intergroup conflicts. There can be no doubt of the value of such conferences, either for learning more about the other group and its leadership or for taking steps, backed by the power of each group, to build mutual trust in dealing with problems that concern them. But our survey of literature led us to suspect that this procedure, unaided by other considerations, would be insufficient to initiate cooperative interaction across group lines.

The reasons may be stated briefly: in order to be a "leader," in any sense other than an autocratic monarch or a dictator with total power over every segment of one's group, an individual must be responsible to pursue the goals of his group within the prevailing bounds for acceptable means. If he transgresses these limits, someone — sooner or later — will expose him as a traitor or as being soft on the adversary. For groups gripped in severe conflict, these bounds of propriety surely include behavior with the out-group, even extending to the point of prescribing personal encounters with the leader of the out-group. (As of this writing, the reader can understand this stricture by imagining the reactions within their countries if either the President of the United States or the Premier of China should propose a joint "summit meeting.") Therefore, we concluded that realistic appraisals of the role of meetings between leaders had to assume that *some* cooperative interaction or some common interests already existed between the groups. This was not the case in our experiments.

Individual competition according to the abilities of persons also has been proposed as a means of furthering intergroup cooperation. In classroom and recreation situations, this measure appears to be used pragmatically to break up groups that adults detect. On a larger scale, we find no evidence that track meets between Negroes and whites, or Olympic games between nations, have materially advanced cooperation between the groups represented by the respective winners and losers.

The hypotheses in regard to these questions were formulated in the light of these considerations.

HYPOTHESES

1. *Contact* between groups on an equal status in activities that, in themselves, are pleasant for members of both

groups, but that involve no interdependence among them, will not decrease an existing state of intergroup conflict.

2. When conflicting groups come into contact under conditions embodying goals *that are compelling for the groups involved, but cannot be achieved by a single group through its own efforts and resources,* the groups will tend to cooperate toward this *superordinate goal.* Our definition of superordinate goal emphasizes that it is unattainable by one group, singly; hence, it is not identical with a "common goal." Another implication of the definition is that a superordinate goal supersedes other goals each group may have, singly or in common with others; hence its attainment may require subordination of either singular or common goals.

3. Cooperation between groups arising from a *series* of superordinate goals will have a cumulative effect toward reducing the social distance between them, changing hostile attitudes and stereotypes, and hence reducing the possibility of future conflicts between them.

It may be seen that the measures actually tested in our experiment were introduced with the objective of clarifying the necessary conditions for *contact as equals* to be effective in reducing existing conflicts between groups and changing attitudes of their members.

PHASE ONE

In order to test the first hypothesis, a series of situations was introduced involving *contact* between groups in activities highly pleasant to each group but not involving interdependence between them. Examples were going to the movies, eating in the same dining room, shooting off fireworks on July 4, and the like. Far from reducing conflict, these situations served as occasions for the rival groups to berate and attack each other. In the dining-hall line, they shoved each other, and the group that lost the contest for the head of the line shouted "Ladies first!" at the winner. They threw paper, food, and vile names at each other. An Eagle bumped by a Rattler was admonished by his fellow Eagles to brush "the dirt" off his clothes. The mealtime encounters were dubbed "garbage wars" by the participants.

The measure that was effective was suggested by a corollary to our assumptions about intergroup conflict: *if conflict develops from mutually incompatible goals, common goals should promote co-operation.* But what kind of common goals?

In considering group relations in the everyday world, it seemed that the most effective and enduring cooperation between groups occurs when *superordinate goals* prevail, superordinate goals being those that have a compelling appeal for members of each group, but that neither group can achieve without participation of the other. To test this hypothesis experimentally, we created a series of urgent and natural situations that challenged individuals in both groups.

One was a breakdown in the water supply system. Water came to the camp in pipes from a tank about a mile away. The flow of water was interrupted and the boys in both groups were called together to hear of the crisis. Both groups promptly volunteered, in their own distinctive ways, to search the water line for trouble. They explored separately, then came together and jointly located the source of the difficulty. But despite the good spirits aroused, the groups fell back on their old recriminations once the immediate crisis was over.

A similar opportunity was offered when the boys requested a movie that both groups had high on their list of preference. They were told that the camp could not afford to pay for it. The two groups got together, figured out how much each group would have to contribute, chose the film by a common vote, and enjoyed the show together. It should be kept in mind that this followed the episode of their cooperation in the water crisis.

One day the two groups went on an outing at a lake some distance away. A large truck was to go for food. But when everyone was hungry and ready to eat, it developed that the truck would not start (the staff had taken care of that). The boys got a rope — the same rope they had used in their acrimonious tug of war — and all pulled together to start the truck.

Joint efforts in situations such as these did not *immediately* dispel hostility. But gradually, the series of activities requiring interdependent action reduced conflict and hostility between the groups. As a consequence, the members of the two groups began to feel friendlier. For example, a Rattler whom the Eagles had disliked for his sharp tongue and skill in defeating them became a "good egg." The boys stopped shoving each other in the meal line. They no longer called each other names and began to sit together at the table. New friendships developed, cutting across group lines.

In the end, the groups were actively seeking opportunities to intermingle, to entertain and "treat" each other. Procedures that "worked" in one activity were *transferred* to others. For example, the notion of "taking turns" developed in the dining hall and was transferred to a joint campfire, which the boys themselves decided to hold. The groups took turns presenting skits and songs.

Given the alternative of returning in separate buses or on the same bus, members of both groups requested that they go home together on the same bus. As a whole neither group paid attention to a few *die-hards* who muttered "Let's not."

On the way home, a stop was made for refreshments. One group still had five dollars won as a prize. They decided to spend this sum on refreshments for both groups, rather than using it solely for themselves and thereby having more to eat. On their own initiative they invited their former rivals to be their guests for malted milks.

Interviews with the boys confirmed the change in their attitudes. From choosing their best friends almost exclusively in their own group, many of them shifted to listing some boys in the other group. They were glad to have a second chance to rate the boys in the other group as to personal qualities. Some remarked that they were inclined to change their minds since the first rating made after the tournament. Indeed they had. The new ratings were largely favorable. It is probably not accidental that the group that had been declared victorious in the intergroup tournament was also more prone to continue attributing negative qualities to the out-group and to remain more exclusive in in-group choices.

CONCLUSIONS

1. Intergroup conflict and its by-products of hostility and negative stereotypes are not *primarily* a result of neurotic tendencies on the part of individuals, but occur under conditions specified here even when the individuals involved are normal, healthy, and socially well adjusted.

2. Cooperative and democratic procedures *within* groups are not directly transferable to intergroup relations. On the contrary, co-

operativeness and solidarity within groups were at their height when intergroup conflict was most severe.

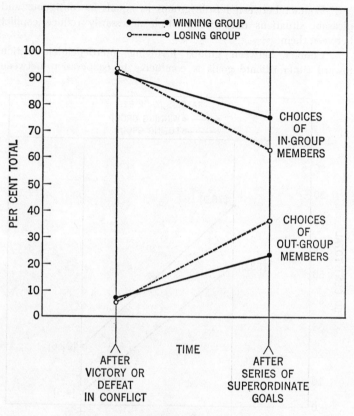

Figure 5.3

Changes in percentage of friendship choices of in-group and out-group members by winning and defeated groups.

3. Important intergroup relations affect the patterning of roles and the norms within each group. As noted earlier, one group deposed a leader who could not "take it" in contests with the adversary. Another made a hero of a big boy who had previously been regarded as a bully. Similarly, the change to intergroup

cooperation was accompanied by shifts in the status structure, particularly in one group in which some members looked back on the former days of rivalry with nostalgia.

4. Contact between hostile groups as equals in contiguous and pleasant situations does not in itself necessarily reduce conflict between them.

5. Contact between groups involving interdependent action toward superordinate goals is conducive to cooperation between

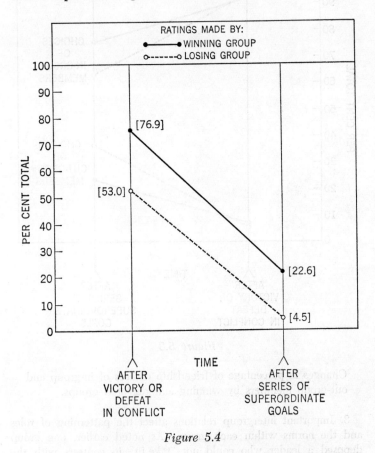

Figure 5.4

Percentage of categorically unfavorable ratings of out-group after intergroup conflict and after series of superordinate goals.

groups, but a single episode of cooperation is not sufficient to reduce established intergroup hostility and negative stereotypes.

6. A series of cooperative activities toward superordinate goals has a cumulative effect in reducing intergroup hostility. This cumulative effect involves the successful development of procedures for cooperating in specific activities and their transfer to new situations, so that established modes of intergroup cooperation are recognized.

7. Tools and techniques found useful in problem-solving within groups and in intergroup conflict may also serve in intergroup cooperation. (In the experiments, the tug-of-war rope was used to pull the stalled truck.) But their use in intergroup cooperation requires recognition that the procedures involve not merely so many individuals within a group, but different groups of individuals contributing to the attainment of a common goal.

8. Cooperative endeavor between groups toward superordinate goals alters the significance of other measures designed to reduce existing hostility between them:

Intergroup *contacts* in the course of striving toward superordinate goals were used for developing plans, for making decisions, and for pleasant exchanges.

Information about the other group became interesting and sought after, rather than something to be ignored or interpreted to fit existing conceptions of the out-group.

Exchange of persons for the performance of tasks was not seen as "betrayal" of one's own group.

Leaders found that the trend toward intergroup cooperation widened the spheres in which they could take positive steps toward working out procedures for joint endeavor and future contact. In fact, a leader who tried to hold back from intergroup contact found that his group was ceasing to listen to him.

In short, the findings suggest that various methods used with limited success in reducing intergroup hostility may become effective when employed within a framework of cooperation among groups working toward goals that are genuinely appealing to all and that require equitable participation and contributions from all groups. The implications of this conclusion for the measures that *can* be effective in reducing intergroup conflict on the larger scene will be discussed in Chapter 8.

6

Verification and Extension of the Experiments

The implication of the popular saying "The proof of the pudding is in the eating" is not to be dismissed lightly in appraising research. Applied to research findings, the proverbial statement implies concern over *validity*, which has been emphasized in several connections in this book.

The last two chapters presented the background and orientation of our research program, delineating the proper domain of the problem area. A guiding generalization concerning the rise of friendly or hostile intergroup attitudes and actions was presented in Chapter 4. From this generalization, specific hypotheses were formulated for experimental testing. The experimental design in successive stages, the problem situations appropriate to conditions in each stage, and techniques for data collection all followed from the orientation to the problem.

Conclusions drawn in the last chapter were based on findings concerning factors *sufficient* for the production of intergroup hostility and the conditions *necessary* for its reduction.

Conceptual tools, research methodology, and inferences from data necessarily involve abstractions. But, if the aim is explanation of concrete events and, eventually, their prediction and control, the researcher cannot remain complacently aloof merely because his work entails abstraction. If he is interested in the *validity* of the abstraction, he must observe the extensions of his findings in appropriate areas of application. Industrial relations, race relations, and international relations are obviously among the crucial areas in which research on intergroup relations may be applied in order to test its validity.

In this chapter, we present extensions and applications of the orientation and findings from the experiments. These all involve relationships of groups *within* nations. In subsequent chapters, some problems *between* nations are examined from the standpoint of this research.

EXTENDING THE EXPERIMENTAL ANALYSIS

Can the experiments on intergroup relations serve as a basis for analyzing conflict and cooperation between groups in actual life? They were designed to test specific hypotheses based on the general formulation of intergroup problems under controlled conditions. Blake and Mouton (1962) refer to the experiments as *prototypes* for analysis. Certainly many variations are possible.

The first question is whether other research verifies or extends the findings through logical inference based upon them. The second concerns whether or not the findings apply to cases in which the persons, power relations, and histories of issues differ substantially from those in the experiments. After all, the subjects in the experiments were young boys; the groups were small and roughly equal in power; the entire history of their encounters lasted a few weeks; unlike some intergroup systems, problems between the groups were not subject to adjudication with common consent by a still higher authority, nor did the research staff intervene to encourage negotiation or arbitration of differences.

Additional Verification of
the Experiments

The obvious site for replicating the sequence of stages in the experiments is a real summer camp. In a field study conducted by Sussman and Weil (1960), two cabins at a camp for diabetic children participated for three days in activities conducive to the formation of tighter in-groups and for a single day in competitive games with prizes offered to the group winning the entire tournament. Even in this short time, a sequence of behavior similar to that in our experiments was observed. During the in-group stage, friendship choices of children outside the cabin were reduced. Following the tournament, friendship preference was directed *within* the group almost exclusively (more than 90 per cent of choices), revealing again the effect of intergroup relations on solidarity within the group. The one-day tournament produced "name-calling, back-biting, recriminations, fighting."

The increase in group solidarity and the rise of hostile attitudes and images also has been reported by Blake and Mouton (1962) among mature adults in workshop situations. It may be concluded that intergroup encounters directed toward objectives whose attainment by one group means their loss by the other are sufficient for the rise of intergroup hostility and antagonistic attitudes. The effects of intergroup conflict on solidarity and the organizational structure of in-groups have also been verified in these studies.

Proceeding from the same formulation of intergroup problems, Avigdor (1952) conducted an experiment in a settlement house among friendship clubs of girls. Her aim was to test the prediction that the stereotyped images that one group develops of another reflect the conflicting or cooperative nature of relations between them. She predicted that the particular traits attributed to the out-group would be those most *relevant* to the in-group's position, whether typifying the actual behavior of the other group or not.

Some clubs cooperated in producing a play whose proceeds were to be spent on club jackets for each group. The members of these cooperating groups were initially neither favorable nor unfavorable in their views of one another. They came to have favorable images that were not strikingly categorical (not as expressed in the phrase "all or most of them are that way"). The groups who had reason to believe that their achievement of club jackets was being blocked by other groups became hostile toward them, attributing highly negative characteristics to them in categorical fashion. There was also evidence that traits irrelevant to the conflict (for example, "bad teeth") were excluded from the negative image. Instead, the image of the transgressors centered around those qualities each group saw as responsible for their joint frustration. The other group was "selfish," "bossy," "cheating."

Young women are not immune to the same processes, as O. J. Harvey (1954) found in his experiment. Friendly cliques held positive images of each other, and assessed the performance by persons in the other cliques about as accurately as they did their own. But unfriendly cliques held unfavorable stereotypes of each other, and downgraded performance by members of the out-group to the point of *under*estimating it. When the unfriendly group was present, each group overestimated its own performance, revealing thereby the tendency to "close ranks" and glorify one's own group in the face of an unfriendly competitor.

An experiment by Manheim (1960) showed that invidious comparisons between groups influenced the proportion of hostile communication between them. Images of another group were created by instructions implying favorable or unfavorable comparisons between the groups. For example, having been told that its average intelligence was low or high, a group was assigned the task of reaching agreement with another group to which the same, a lower or higher intelligence, was attributed. Manheim found that the proportion of negative and antagonistic expressions in notes passed between the groups increased (relative to the total) as the number of invidious comparisons in their images of each other increased. The greatest proportion of hostile communications occurred between groups who differed both in their images of each other's intelligence and of the relative autonomy or authoritarian character of each other's leadership.

In an exploratory study in a vacation settlement, Jamous and LeMaine (1962) report striking effects upon the structure, activities, and satisfaction within groups competing toward a prize with unequal facilities for the tasks at hand. As the authors observed, possession of differential facilities and resources is characteristic of relations between many groups in actual life. In their research, groups of children (ages nine to fourteen) competed in three different types of activities (decoding instructions and using them to build an object, constructing a shelter in the woods, and planning an ideal vacation camp). For each task, one group had inferior means at its disposal, either through lack of information and materials, or difference in age.

Not surprisingly, some of the less favored groups became discouraged and did not want to compete. But it was clear that competition between the favored and handicapped groups resulted in very different atmospheres within them: the handicapped groups had more interpersonal friction, greater difficulties in dividing the work, frequent struggles for status, and differing attitudes toward the other group. Notably, the favored groups were quite open in allowing others to see their work and in wishing to compare it with that of the other group. The handicapped groups tended to "close their frontiers" to prevent comparison.

None of the studies just reviewed attempted reduction of inter-group hostility. Studies of intergroup conflict in industry and race relations will provide an opportunity to clarify the conditions and variations that must be considered in reducing existing hostility between groups.

Intergroup Relations in Industrial Settings

A number of investigators have analyzed conflicts within indus-trial organizations in terms of intergroup relations (e.g., Whyte, 1955; Blake and Mouton, 1962; Blake, Shepard, and Mouton, 1964; Lawrence *et al.*, 1961). The workshop experiments of Blake and Mouton, in particular, provide verification of our experiments among sophisticated adults attending workshops on human relations problems.

Experimental Verification with Adults. In summaries of a series of separate reports (Blake and Mouton, 1962; Blake, Shepard, and Mouton, 1964), the investigators report the formation of group structures in workshops, the production of intergroup hostility and unfavorable images following a series of competitive encounters between groups on a "win or lose" basis, the heightened solidarity and self-glorification of the in-group during conflict, and the effects of the latter upon individual perception and judgment of performance. Since these findings for mature adults in workshop settings are basically similar to those in our experiments, the focus here will be upon the extensions made by these investigators during thirty workshops with a total of about one thousand participants, all adults.

Once workshop groups began to take shape after ten to eighteen hours of in-group activity, they were assigned tasks such as dis-cussing problems in human relations to formulate the "best" solu-tion they could reach. During interaction aimed at reaching a "better" solution than a competing group could offer, the rather loose and incipient power (status) relations within each group were "refined" and "consolidated." Groups closed ranks to pull together cohesively to *win;* bickering among members diminished.

Interaction *between* groups was studied in several ways, each revolving around the decision as to which group's performance (proposed solution) was superior. In one procedure, each group chose members to represent it in negotiations for a common choice between proposals. Before these negotiations began, persons in both groups agreed that all the negotiators chosen were "mature, intelligent, independent, and well-intentioned." During negotiations, each group could send notes to instruct its own representative or to request him to secure more information about the other group's proposal. When these notes were analyzed, it was found that very little effort had been made to clarify similarities and differences in the proposals. Rather, the notes reflected attempts to poke holes in the rival proposals and to belittle the rival's efforts, even though the notes were written by mature adults at a workshop designed to improve their understanding of human behavior.

Once representatives reached a common decision on the proposals, the reactions of adult members to them were striking. Persons in the losing group now regarded representatives of the other group as less intelligent, less mature, and less well intentioned than formerly. While their own representative had been seen as bravely defending their proposal, he was seen as a *traitor* if he agreed too readily to the rival's solution. If, on the other hand, he emerged with the award, he received a hero's welcome.

A neutral "third party" brought in to adjudicate the decision fared little better. Initially, both sides agreed that the third party was neutral and competent to decide between the proposals. The winning group took his decision as evidence that "we were *right*." Losing groups saw the erstwhile neutral as "biased, unfair, incompetent"; with "no grasp of the problem"; "not intelligent enough to be fair and unbiased"; not knowing "enough about the topic"; not taking "enough time" to reach a good decision.

Objective tests given to members of each group about the two proposals revealed the tendency in each group to recognize the distinctive points in its own proposals and to *claim* as its own many elements that were actually *common* to both groups. In other words, the categorical distinction between groups hindered discrimination of similarities actually present in the proposals.

In the workshop situations, the winning groups experienced the glow of victory, but were unable to appreciate why the losing group should be at all disturbed about losing. Losing groups were subdued and gloomy, usually turning to see why they lost. Initial blaming of the decision-makers was sometimes followed by self-criticism initiated by members who had not been strongly attached to the group's proposal in the first place and who could now speak out critically. The usual result was considerable disorganization and splintering within some of the defeated groups. New leadership sometimes emerged during the ensuing in-group discussion about the defeat.

Following these events, the workshops introduced various procedures aimed at showing the participants how their feelings and actions sprang from the intergroup relations and providing planned experiences to avoid their repetition during joint analysis and solution of problems by groups and their representatives. The investigators reported several interesting cases suggesting the effectiveness of the training procedures in business in resolving interdepartmental conflicts, headquarter-branch antagonisms, and problems of mergers (Blake, Shepard, and Mouton, 1964). Such procedures can be effective when they highlight common interests that are sufficiently strong to override antagonisms and point toward practical ways of cooperating toward those interests. This is the essential condition required in the concept of superordinate goals.

Reduction of Conflict in Industrial Organizations

In discussing superordinate goals in industrial settings, it is important to specify differences from the model of our experiments. Obviously, the participants are adults going about the vital business of production and earning a living in a large organization. Another notable difference is that relations between groups in industry are regulated by larger authorities: relations between departments by higher management; dealings between labor and management by contractual agreements and government regulation; and relations between establishments by certain laws. Another salient difference is that some groups in industry possess notably more power than others. The kind of power available to each also differs.

Under these circumstances, the methods of dealing with intergroup conflicts have seldom involved superordinate goals. More frequently, the methods have been exertion of one's power to force settlement, bargaining under threat of force by one or both sides, intervention by a higher authority, or long-term attempts at persuasion and reward to get one group to subordinate its goals to those of another (as when a management attempts to convince a union organization that its best interests are served by identifying with company policy).

As long as various groups have objectives that are, in fact, conflicting and adopt all-or-nothing positions, the application or threat of force may lead to quiescence or an uneasy "peace"; but it does not provide the motivational basis for recurrent cooperation. Force or coercion do not represent superordinate goals. Their results are reminiscent of the old saying, "You can lead a horse to water but you can't make him drink."

Since genuine conflicts of interest are very real in community and national life, the question of the nature and relevance of superordinate goals in industrial settings is particularly interesting. A case in point was reported in Lawrence *et al.* (1961, pp. 452–472) involving departments with fairly equal power, each with legitimate but rival claims bringing a new product into manufacture for their company. The industrial engineers regarded the design as "ours," to the chagrin of the development engineers. The industrial engineers became convinced that the development engineers were out to block production of the product. The production manager was simply puzzled, commenting that everyone was mad and touchy.

Plans for production broke down so badly that top management began to consider withdrawing the product. This common threat brought the two engineering groups together for the first time in cooperative efforts to "save" the product. Production of the article represented a superordinate goal that both sides desired strongly, that required their cooperative efforts and subordination of rival claims over a period of time. Afterward, persons on each side reported that during these joint experiences they each began to appreciate, for the first time, the problems faced by their erstwhile rivals.

Such cases differ from the usual conflict involving management and labor groups in industry. The early history of labor-management relations in this country is a chronicle of repeated collective clashes between workers determined to alleviate and improve their conditions and owners or managers adamantly resisting or crushing these efforts. Indeed, the origins of union and management groups as organized entities lie in such encounters. It is no accident that the rise of hostile attitudes and negative stereotypes in union-management history resembles that in the intergroup experiments, for we were well aware of the events when the studies were designed.

Currently, however, labor-management relations in this country have become more institutionalized through regulation toward certain "core objectives" supported by both sides, albeit for different reasons. These characteristics, as Dubin (1962) has shown, are the earmarks of an intergroup system, stabilized in some degree for the time. When one side or another focuses on incompatible aims and takes an all-or-nothing stand, the sequence of threat of force and actual force can only lead to open conflict or forced settlement. Within the *modus vivendi* reached, writes Dubin, the specific purposes of labor and management limit the alternatives that leaders on either side can consider for resolving conflicts. The intergroup system as it exists requires that leadership on both sides take into account the limitations placed on each side by its own organization, if open splits are to be avoided.

Within this framework of labor-management relations, a broad motivational basis for cooperation does sometimes emerge toward core objectives supported by both sides, even though for different reasons. In the very interesting cases reported by Blake and Mouton (1962) and Blake, Shepard, and Mouton (1964), several management and union groups desired to avoid further conflict that hindered their pursuit of core objectives and made negotiations of routine differences more difficult. Although the heavy hand of past disputes and modes of dealing with them slowed their efforts in varying degrees, such groups did work out more fruitful procedures for negotiation with the guidance of consultants acceptable to both sides.

In one case, management alone took the initiative to avoid conflict and the consultants worked through management. One point at issue was management's acceptance of the union (an international union), whose leaders believed with some justification that the company preferred a company or independent union. With the identity of one party at stake, the managers' unilateral determination to offer opportunities for cooperation and *not* to regard the union as an "enemy" was repeatedly shaken. In such cases, the investigators concluded, the emergence of superordinate goals probably awaits opportunities for the union to test management's avowed intent to "get along." The opportunity for cooperative union-management relations hinges upon development of *new* issues, unsullied by the older antagonisms that gave rise to the mutually hostile images so closely connected with the identity of one of the parties.

Application to the Civil Rights Issue

The most visible area of intergroup conflicts within the United States, especially during the past decade, has been the struggle for civil rights by Negro citizens. More recently the struggle has broadened into movements aimed at social and economic opportunity for all underprivileged citizens, including the disproportionate share that are Negroes.

The extent of segregation and lack of opportunity in American life were revealed to Americans and the rest of the world by the turn of events, roughly after 1954, belying the prior quietude that had persisted despite the sporadic lynchings and mob violence. Both the outraged cries of avowed segregationists and the puzzled surprise of avowed moderates over the "new Negro" revealed lack of insight into the Negro condition and the poverty of communication between white and Negro citizens. The lost status of erstwhile Negro leaders, who had risen to leadership positions through accommodating to the local citadels of white power, revealed the peculiar combination of force and submission to force required by prevailing arrangements (Killian, 1962).

Protests, initiated by middle-class students and spreading throughout the country, were made in the nonviolent terms formulated by Gandhi, who had faced the even more overwhelming power of the British in India. Like Gandhi's efforts, nonviolent resistance brought retaliation, adamant resistance, and counterforce from those who possessed power or were unafraid of the sources of power. Here the similarities end.

In this country, both the duly constituted federal government and the sympathies of many white citizens were on the side of the demonstrators. The demonstrators, in turn, pressed toward "our rightful" places within the American system of life, changed though it might be by their inclusion. Both national and local levels were aware that local protests would have an impact on other parts of the country and on the international scene.

For such reasons, unlike the Indian movement which had to endure half a century of oppression and postponement, the civil rights demonstrations with the more limited aims exemplified in sit-ins and boycotts began to produce results before the eyes of the participants. The results were not always or even usually exactly what had been requested. Yet there seems to be no doubt that demonstrations and campaigns, with their ensuing experiences of imprisonment and violence for the protesters, were an essential condition for any change to occur in the foreseeable future.

In this discussion, our interest lies in the question of *how* the changes came about, once the protests were made. Recently, Jones and Long (1965) completed an analysis of desegregation decisions in ten of the largest cities in the southern United States, varying in size from 80,000 to 1,000,000, with only two having fewer than 100,000 persons. The changes in these cities, they found, did not "just happen." They followed a pattern of crisis, with some form of open conflict, whose resolution was the result of settlements worked out by people who urgently recognized the need for steps "that would prove creative rather than destructive in their communities" (p. 3).

The *impetus* for change, they concluded, must give

> . . . full and due credit to the young direct actionists. What changes have come in the South have been determined in the courts and in the streets, usually due to both the establishment of legal prerogative *and* direct mass action. *How* these changes came about has been the result of negotiation. However, few of the young direct actionists have participated in the implementation of the changes their demands have won (p. 15).

Jones and Long found that desegregation of public facilities had not been undertaken voluntarily by public officials in any of the cities. In the instances in which voluntary efforts were claimed, the threat of protests had been clear and present. In fact, they comment that "municipal authorities needed the appearance of being forced to act to prevent application of counter forces by segregationists" (p. 13). In most cities, the negotiations were conducted without benefit of official presence, although many of the committees were established by the city governments.

Jones and Long studied the negotiators in the ten cities, their backgrounds, the circumstances of negotiation, and reactions to the outcomes. They found that, with local variations, negotiators in all cities were persons who undertook the task and could pursue hitherto unconventional alternatives because, *for different reasons,* they perceived objectives superordinate to the immediate claims of the demonstrators and to the counterclaims of most white persons in the community, including many of their friends and associates.

The characteristics of the negotiators are particularly interesting. They were persons "respected on their own side of the color line and . . . across the line" (p. 59), though not primarily for direct involvement for or against desegregation. In the case of Negro members, this meant that the most active and prestigious leaders of action organizations were not included, a fact that brought criticism from demonstration leaders, but not condemnation of the Negro negotiators. None of the latter was accused of betraying his people.

The typical negotiator was over forty years old, a college graduate following a profession (other than the ministry) or in business, born in an upper Southern or border state, had lived in the city in which negotiations occurred for ten or more years, and had participated in a large number of community and professional organizations, including interracial religious organizations. Some 40 per cent of the white negotiators had lived outside the South at some time.

The limitations placed upon negotiators by virtue of their membership in their communities are shown most clearly by the frequent insistence that their names and affiliations not be revealed publicly even after negotiations were completed. For somewhat different reasons, negotiators in several cities secured cooperation from the mass media not to make public announcements of planned settlements until after desegregation steps actually were put into effect. This policy was designed to prevent opposing segregationists from arriving on the scene before desegregation was accomplished.

The goals that brought and kept the negotiators working were, as noted, diverse. They included "personal philosophy, religious faith, business policy, and political expediency" (p. 60). In each city, however, the overriding consideration to negotiators was to avert the crisis or threat of crisis to their city, regarded as certain if inaction were the course. Thus, the common focus was "what is good" for the community. Their perspectives on what was good for the community had, in many cases, been shaped by participation as professionals and businessmen in mass production and distribution activities of the larger economy with the "personnel and customer relations that these imply: uniformity and interchangeability."

The authors suggest that the changes that occurred in the ten cities, although many were of a "token" nature compared to the ultimate objectives of action groups, are nevertheless significant. They provide a setting more conducive to further social change. They demonstrate both the limitations of public leadership and the possibilities of negotiation backed by community power and conducted by respected representatives who are sufficiently free of alignments to seek new and creative alternatives to old issues.

The importance of superordinate goals supported by persons not rigidly bound by overriding commitments to the established stand of a single group may be seen in the many communities in which interracial committees have failed through lack of communication or creeping indifference (cf. Killian and Grigg, 1964). For example, in one community in which open strife had not been the rule, the best intentions of committee members bogged down and eventually failed to secure joint agreements toward changing the situation. The limited accomplishment was shown in the fact that only the Negro members thought the committee needed to continue its work. Though of good will, the white members lacked feelings of compelling urgency to continue. The authors also stress the importance of superordinate goals as the necessary condition for good will to be translated into decisions to try new and viable alternatives in human relations.

In this changing world, there are people of good will who genuinely desire to redress old wrongs and to facilitate change in equitable directions. Too often, good will bogs down in a morass of old arrangements and emotional smarts. The translation of good will into action requires give-and-take among persons who have lived their lives in group contexts designed for domination or submission, suppression or rebellion. Similar problems are found in new nations composed of traditional divisions, different tribes, religions, language, or ethnic groupings.

Modern India, with its constitution barring religious or caste discrimination and providing legal compensatory opportunities for the disadvantaged, has experienced a resurgence of caste and religious lines despite its stated national goals. It is noteworthy that two analysts of the Indian scene, one studying religious conflict (Ram, 1955) and one, caste (Sinha, 1961), have concluded that a series of superordinate goals is necessary for the changes intended by their constitution. In a vast country, such goals need to be translated to each locality and people so that procedures to implement them can be developed. These are preliminary to the transformation in outlook required to sustain the persistent effort toward the goals.

As all the foregoing authorities have noted, there is an alternative to initiating broadly motivated efforts toward changing human relations: prolonged crisis between groups in conflict. During prolonged crises, there is always the distinct possibility that people will be aroused by joint deprivation and frustration, but not be at all responsive to the leadership of organized groups or the community. The irresponsible leader of a destructive mob or the demagogue moved chiefly by personal gain holds sway when no segment of society takes responsibility for the consequences of its actions, and none can set forth goals that can unite the dissident group.

In such cases, the crisis becomes a clash between peoples bent on destruction. The expenditure of life and human effort in such crises is tragic because it is not directed toward changing the circumstances that produce the crisis nor toward changing the relationships that produce conflict.

Criteria of Superordinate Goals

Members of groups in conflict may see wisdom in avoiding alternatives that offer only destruction and counterdestruction. Unless the goal of one group is annihilation or exploitation of the other, there are possibilities of superordinate goals in various spheres of activity. If the efficacy of such goals is to be tested, they must be based on conditions in which all groups, regardless of their positions of power or powerlessness, desire objectives that require contributions from all according to their resources and potential effort. They must be sufficiently compelling so that each group pursues them without coercion in the form of violence or its threat. Such conditions are conducive to cooperative efforts between groups, during which each group may willingly subordinate certain of its claims for a time. But, it is unrealistic to assume that any group will subordinate claims that represent the most pressing of its members' dreams, whether these be for good or ill.

On the contrary, superordinate goals are possible only when two or more groups find a purpose toward which each can strive without sacrificing the most cherished aspirations of its members. When this is not possible, group conflict continues despite efforts to forestall its ultimate consequences and despite practices that appear legitimate to each group. Some of the practices that have proven sterile in reduction of group conflict are discussed in the next chapter.

7

Traditional Ways of Dealing with Intergroup Problems: Casting Blame and Deterrence

If the findings and conclusions drawn from research are valid, they should provide some guides to decision about practical measures. The research on intergroup relations should yield at least general orientations about what will be fruitful and what will be sterile in dealing effectively with problems of intergroup hostility.

In this chapter, two traditional practices in dealing with intergroup conflicts are scrutinized. These particular practices were selected because they are common and because our research shows reasons why they further complicate intergroup problems, rather than cope with them effectively.

The first is that of assigning blame for intergroup conflict. The second involves assessing the adversary's strength with the objective of forestalling violence through preparedness or offensive posture. This orientation currently appears under the title of the *deterrence formula,* which is the new label for the old "balance of power" policy.

Measures that do have potentialities for reducing or solving problems of groups in conflict are discussed in Chapter 8.

WHO'S TO BLAME?

It is not difficult to understand why parties in conflict want to establish who is to blame for hostility and violence. What actually happens in a search for culprits is not so easily understood.

Of course human beings, not the clubs or guns or bombs they use, bear responsibility for intergroup violence. The human intellect is capable of studying events to analyze human responsibility for the course intergroup relations takes. If conflicting groups willingly submit to a higher authority with the agreement to abide by its judgment, open conflict sometimes can be avoided. In such "settlements," too, assignment of blame seldom reduces existing hostility between groups; indeed, it may provide the impetus for intensified hatred. As a *solution* to intergroup conflict, the assessment of blame is never more than a first step. Without mutual agreement on this step, the query "Who's to blame?" invariably leads to a vicious circle of recriminations that intensify conflict.

Every normal human adult spends a good part of his intellectual activity assessing causation of events, especially if the events are in any way disturbing or unusual. Disturbing or unusual events involving other groups become topics of concern and discussion when they are related to the successes, failures, victories, or defeats of one's own group. To account for their successes and failures, human groups have used every imaginable etiology devised by man, including geography, climate, the actions of third parties, resources, heredity, fate, and deities (cf. Shafer, 1955). These have been translated into causes affecting people *within their own* groups and people *within other* groups.

When a group is in conflict with another, several compelling circumstances militate toward highly selective and incomplete evaluation of itself and the opponent. In ardent pursuit of their own aims, the members are likely to see and appraise events entirely as these bear on their aims. If conflict is intense and prolonged, ways of learning about or communicating with the other group become limited. The antagonist, seen at peaks of conflict when representing his own group, is appraised on the basis of his behavior *at that moment*.

Thus, as our intergroup experiments showed, the assignment of blame is conducted almost entirely from the in-group's point of view (Chapters 5 and 6). The adversary's behavior, which is not usually the behavior *we* intended to provoke, is regarded as *his* responsibility and is not easily forgiven. At the peak of intergroup violence, determination of responsibility may be almost impossible, even for impartial observers. There is still no agreement among several trained observers as to which group started the first "garbage war" in the dining hall (Chapter 5).

Blinding Effects of Group Images

Stereotyped images arising during prolonged intergroup conflict are typically descriptions that both assign blame to the group and vindicate the motives of one's own group. When we have publicly dubbed a people as an "enemy," their persistent pursuit of their own ends in a bargaining session is "evidence" that they are *cold* and *calculating*, which justifies our conclusion that there is no point in trying to negotiate.

To many white Americans, Negroes occupy their status precisely because they "are" uneducated, poverty stricken, superstitious, disease ridden. Then some of these white Americans reveal the relative importance they assign to color and citizenship in their society by bestowing upon the fraction of educated Negroes the task of "improving the image" of the Negro people. Certainly this is a Herculean task when one remembers that large numbers of their white brethren project images that they would be reluctant to assume responsibility for "improving."

In Chapter 2, the ossifying effect of race doctrine upon intergroup images was discussed. In more modern garb, images of other peoples phrased in substantive categories are equally stultifying. Taking a given people and their history as we see it, the attributes assigned to them both justify events of the past, current problems, and future forecasts.

Examples are easy to find: the assessments of American colonists by British aristocrats and their subsequent view of the new nation; the images of the revolutionaries by much of the European world at the time of the French Revolution; predictions about the longevity and viability of the Soviet Union that persisted even after World War II; year-to-year forecasts by Europeans of the internal collapse of newly formed Asian nations. These are but a few instances in which the substantive assessment depicted an incomplete historical account, assigned blame for contemporary events to the peoples in question, concluded that their proposed solution was impossible, and predicted failure or catastrophe.

Today, such substantive assessment has reached classic proportions in the views within many Western countries of the newly emerging African nations. In these Western eyes, the clouds of racist doctrine drift above icebergs of the "white man's civilizing burden." Below the surface are the very real interests that have kept white men in Africa in recent centuries and make them reluctant to relinquish control over its fate. Through such eyes, the state of things at a given moment is an absolute portent of the future.

They hold that Africa's alien ways, poverty-stricken peoples, unspeakable differences in ways of living, paucity of persons trained in modern administration and technology are a result of the African's tastes and preferences, certainly not of the courageous persistence of white people in Africa. In this view, the African nation cannot succeed because its people fundamentally lack the necessary interests and aspirations.

The following excerpts from an article on the "White Man's Future in Black Africa" were written by a former career diplomat turned journalist, whose account is not lacking in evidence of good will toward Africans (Stevens, 1960). First, the history:

> It took 100 years of white rule to rouse the African from the torpor in which he had always existed. The white man built the roads, railways, and eventually the airports. . . . He developed the agricultural and mineral resources, and even provided the education from which sprouted the tree of independence. The African — talented though he is in music, art, and, be it frankly admitted, politics — contributed nothing to this development but his labor (pp. 60–61).

This historical account, which reads more like the history of a business than an account of the conquest of peoples, makes it difficult to understand why Africans ever wanted independence. The author's assessment of African abilities follows logically from it:

> The unanimous testimony of white management — some of it very sympathetic to African aspirations — is that the African will not accept responsibility. If he had shown the drive and the aptitude, the opportunity would have been forthcoming. . . . The simple fact is that the African displays neither taste nor talent for trade (p. 61).

Africans *are* accepting and taking responsibility into their own hands when they establish new nations, including the responsibility to decide whether establishments within their bounds shall be managed by citizens or foreigners and under what circumstances. They take responsibility for the successes or failures that follow. The writings of their own leaders show that they have different views of their past and their potentialities. Whether or not they succeed, their struggle to relieve the white man of his alleged burden indicates flaws in the analysis that insists the white man is responsible for their future.

CASTING BLAME IN INTERGROUP NEGOTIATIONS

In specific situations in which the representatives of one group face those of another, each with ingrained images of the other's *nature,* the assignment of blame becomes hopelessly entangled with these images. Even though a group may seek self-examination and criticisms within its own bounds, a representative or leader is ordinarily constrained in revealing self-criticism in intergroup encounters. In this country, this tendency has been elevated to the policy level, such that members of rival political parties are expected to subordinate their party's criticism of the country when dealing with another country.

There are further difficulties. Once a party with a well-ingrained conception of his opponent enters negotiations, it is almost impossible for him to conceal this conception consistently. His manner, the questions he asks, and his reactions are colored by it.

Blake, Shepard, and Mouton (1964) report a prolonged session between union and management representatives in which each side participated solely to try to agree on a typical picture of their usual attitudes and modes of dealing with each other, with no technical or substantive issues being considered. The union and management in this case had a history of highly conflicting relationships. The agreement to participate was one evidence of an interest in changing this state of affairs. Yet time after time, representatives of both sides antagonized one another by the way they framed questions and responded to the other's statements.

Here are some excerpts of management representatives' remarks just after leaving the union:

> "I told you! Anything he (the business agent) said, the others would back up. Those guys don't even know what is fact and what is fiction." . . . How could they be so wrong?"

. . . "I think they really know. . . . It fits everything they do. They always use this tactic. We're always the 'scheming' ones and *they* are the 'innocent' ones. The business agent has been to the International's school. They taught him all the tricks" (p. 180).

Among the union representatives, the following remarks were made: "How can they honestly think that we are a clique running our organization?" "The whole problem . . . is that they are still living in the 19th century. They can't understand that unions are here to stay. They have no concept of the ideology of unions" (p. 181).

Without any change in the situation, of course, each side behaves in ways congruent with its own conceptions and sees the behavior of the others as confirming its own ideas. In this connection, the Chairman of the Foreign Relations Committee of the United States Senate, J. William Fulbright, wrote about the effects of preconceptions in international negotiations:

> We must remember that we are not dealing with automatons whose sole function in life is to embody an ideology and a party line, but with human beings — people who, like ourselves, have special areas of pride, prejudice, and sensitivity. I have found, for example, as have others who have discussed current issues with Soviet officials and citizens, that the whole trend of a conversation can be influenced by the way in which you begin it. If you confront them at the outset with an attack on the harshness of their ideology, the shortcomings of their economy, or the excesses of their dictatorship, you are likely to be rewarded with an outburst of chauvinism and vituperation about American policy and practices. There are those who find such encounters emotionally satisfying, but no one can deny that they are singularly barren of productive results.
>
> If, on the other hand, you start out with a compliment about the successes of Soviet society — and there have been a few — or with a candid reference to the shortcomings of our own society — and there have also been a few of these — then it often happens that the response is surprisingly expansive and conciliatory. You are likely to hear an admission that everything, after all, is not perfect in the Soviet Union, and that there are even a few things about America that are admirable and worthy of imitation.

The compliments in themselves are of little importance. But the candor and the cordiality are of great importance. As any good businessman knows, they set a tone and an atmosphere in which emotion gives way to reason and it becomes possible to do business, to move on from cordial generalities to specific negotiations. They generate that minimum of mutual confidence which is absolutely essential for reaching concrete agreements (1964, pp. 73–74).

Blame-Casting as Strategy

To those who see a panacea for intergroup or international discord in assigning blame, it is well to remember that this practice has in the past been extremely effective in sowing new discord and perpetuating the old. Recalling the early days of the independence movement in India, Nehru (1941) wrote of the futility with which the Indians blamed the government, the communalists, and other Indian groups for failures, forgetting that "divide and rule" was the most successful weapon the colonialist government had for maintaining itself (p. 114).

In a very different setting, the southern United States today, assigning blame has taken a similar turn. In this case, the white Southerner is divided from his fellows, white and black, to preserve the segregationist rule. A Southern novelist, Lillian Smith, phrases it in this way:

> We need someone to blame. We cannot bear our anguish if we know it springs from our own hearts. We look around; some name our own U.S. Supreme Court as the mortal enemy; others blame "the North" or the National Association for the Advancement of Colored People or the Communists. But besides ourselves, we can blame the immediate trouble today on the demagogues (the racist politicians) and the ghosts which the demagogues whistle back. . . . Now they are sent forth as maenads by the demagogues to cut the head off of every Orphic truth, to whip and lash every one who dares to disagree, to speak what is right, to measure and examine reality (1964, p. 271).

So it happens that men dare not speak to men about issues that trouble them all, or risk identification with one of the despised "outsiders who are to blame for trouble," with the physical risks such identification sometimes involves.

The consequences of glib appraisals of "who is to blame" are grim today in a world of nations equipped to employ means that promise holocaust to large populations and destruction to portions of the planet for generations to come. On the national level, men have not yet devised a scheme to avoid the awful possibilities. Why should these same men pretend omniscience to pronounce who is to blame for all their difficulties? Yet much of the daily fare in the mass media indulges in this practice.

In this connection, it is well to heed the caution sounded to those who may think any group lily-white and blameless in its dealings by the distinguished psychologist, Charles E. Osgood. Noting that differences between peoples overlay a fundamental humanity that is too often ignored in concern over cultural and ideological differences, he then asked what bearing this fundamental humanity has on the assessment of peoples and their guilt:

> But what about the Russians and the Chinese? There is certainly no reason to believe them deviant from the rest of humanity simply because they adhere to a Communist ideology. Basic modes of human thinking and behaving do not change in chameleon-like fashion as people shift from being our allies to being our enemies and vice versa. There are Russians of the same stock, and Chinese of the same stock, who are not Communist, along with those who are . . .
>
> I realize that . . . there were bloodbaths during the early days of their revolution and there have been some violent purges since then; there was the ruthless stamping down of resistance in Hungary; there are salt mines in Siberia; and there have been executions of men like Nagy. It is to be regretted that men can be inhumanly cruel to other men, but this is a potentiality in all of us. The Russians would point to the sadism and the cruelty of the Germans whom we are now rearming; they would claim that the Hungarian revolt was Capitalist-inspired; and they would ask about the beam in our own eye: our massacres of whole Indian villages, our use of atomic bombs against Japanese civilian centers, the racial violence going on right now in some of our cities. True, we have explanations for these things, but they are just as blind to our justifications as we are to theirs (1962, pp. 138–139).

As long as groups are in conflict, the casting of blame by either side will lead to a vicious circle of mutual recriminations. If they genuinely desire to avoid clashes of armed destruction, the sure course is to seek ways for reducing conflict to a level at which each may pursue legitimate goals that do not infringe upon the others. One by-product of the search is, necessarily, breaking the vicious circle of continual self-justification and mote-casting, which deepens the gulfs between them.

DETERRENCE AS A MEANS OF CIRCUMVENTING VIOLENT CONFRONTATIONS

For well over a century, the orthodox formula has equated peace with a balance of power among nations. If a balance of power were achieved, so went the dogma, each nation could pursue its course unimpeded by war since that nation or its allies would possess resources and weaponry to deter its rivals from resorting to force of arms.

The various concepts of deterrence current today are based on the "balance of power" formula. "Stabilized" deterrence represents the idealized equation of military power. The trappings are modern, of course, replete with jargon derived from mathematical models of games, formal economic theory, computer technology, military strategy, and modern weaponry. Nevertheless, deterrence is the same rancorous weed that flourished before so many disputes and wars in the past.

It is fitting, therefore, to examine the formula in the light of past experiences. In practice, the equation of power required for "balance" was not achieved. Instead, the world witnessed great powers uneasily eyeing one another's weapons, navy, and army, then boasting their "preparedness" to be sure that they *exceeded* the rivals. One mathematician who became interested in the balance formula calculated that a possibility of balance among the European powers was foregone as early as 1908 (Richardson, as quoted by Boulding, 1962).

The continual struggle for hegemony in armed might blossomed into the famous arms races preceding World Wars I and II, justified within each country in the name of "preparedness" and peaceful intent. It is ironic that the most infamous aggressions in history have been associated with slogans like *"Friede durch Macht,"* "Peace Through Strength," or "Peace Through Preparedness," by armies trained with the mission to "keep the peace."

Today the balance of power formula has, as Osgood emphasized, become a formula for balancing terror, owing to the fantastic and awesome capabilities of thermonuclear power and rocketry applied to destructive weapons. C. N. Barclay, British military author, stated the case in the *New York Times Magazine:*

> The deterrent is the modern version of the balance of power, employed in the past — not very successfully — to keep the peace in Europe. The difference lies in the fact that failure to keep the peace in the days of conventional weapons . . . was not universally fatal. Failure with nuclear weapons, on the other hand, would be catastrophic for all mankind (1963, p. 17).

The Fatal Error in Deterrence Concepts

In an age in which space rockets are controlled by electronic means, tremendous prestige accrues to any theory presented as a formal model capable of prediction from computerized information. As a result, concepts of deterrence have spread through the national life from highest officialdom to the reader of the daily paper, whose columns are larded with its jargon. For this reason, some of the most valuable analyses of intergroup conflicts in recent years have concerned the "fit" between assumptions of formal mathematical models adopted by the strategists of deterrence and the characteristics of real conflicts between human groupings (Boulding, 1962; Rappaport, 1960, 1964).

On the whole, formal decision theories have dealt very little with empirical research on actual group conflict. They have documented the potential usefulness of formal models for analysis of group conflict, although the data available for analysis are inadequate. More tellingly, they have revealed the fatal errors in uncritical application of the formal models to practical decision-making.

The fatal errors in application of formal models of the deterrent concept cannot be repaired by greater sophistication, elaboration of the models, or better computers. Nor are the fundamental errors in deterrent theories solely matters of the ethical choice among alternatives, although human beings had best look into their moral pretensions when it becomes almost a parlor game to make guesses about the probable number of human deaths "acceptable" to this or that country.

The fatal errors in the mathematical and economic models, as well as the tragic blunder inherent in deterrent concepts, are of the same order. They result from appalling ignorance of the social psychology of man's behavior in groups. Osgood (1962), writing as an experimental psychologist, grasped this flaw when he wrote "deterrence is more a psychological question than a technological answer" (p. 54).

In discussing formal models of decision theory, Rappaport (1960, p. 359) deplored the lacunae in knowledge on the "psychology of hatred." Later, after surveying the most sophisticated of the strategists, he dubbed the "paucity of psychological knowledge among strategic thinkers" appalling, suggesting that they modeled "life after the maxims of Clausewitz," the German military strategist (1964). It is true that psychology is still in a formative stage as a science, but there are empirical data bearing on the fatal flaws in deterrence theory. For this problem, we need refer only to the way man actually functions when faced with situations in which he and his group are pitted against another group, each eyeing the power of the other relative to his own.

Deterrence Assumptions and Human Behavior Compared

Deterrence concepts all assume that one is facing an enemy whose intent is hostile. It is further assumed that the outbreak of violence can be avoided if one or the other can amass superior capabilities to threaten the opponent or if the two are evenly matched. Since group conflict is seldom a one-shot affair but proceeds over time, the success of the endeavor must assume that each side has some more or less clear ordering of values (or the relative importance of various issues) that remains the same over time. Each side must apprehend both its own preferences and those of the opponent. This information is basic in determining what constitutes a threat and on what issues each group will be adamant. The threat of annihilation is not, after all, always feasible since it can be carried out only once. Stability of deterrence assumes that each side can quite accurately assess the opponent's capabilities to injure and the seriousness of his intent to carry out threats.

But we have already seen that the images of groups in conflict are invariably built from the viewpoint of each in-group in its concerns vis à vis the other group. When the other group is labeled "enemy," the host of traits and prognostications of intent polarized around that label affect present perception and the information that is selected for the computer. Predictions of future intent and of probable reactions to threat are inevitably hazardous because of this inadequate diagnosis of the past and present. Lack of communication between groups further hinders accurate prediction.

Studies of human judgment have shown time and again that even a moderate statement of an opponent's position on a particular issue is appraised by group members as more extreme than it is. As noted in Chapter 2, this peculiar distortion occurs through a contrast effect, in which the difference between the out-group's position and one's own is exaggerated. Similarities are obscured. There is no guarantee that you and your opponent will agree on how aggressive a particular action is, or on whether or not a threat was intended, much less on whether the threat was warranted.

The principles of human judgment are such that an "enemy" who is inferior to us in power is seen as more inadequate than he is; but the minute he begins to approach our power, his power is seen as equal or greater than our own. This is no description of paranoids or hospital cases. It is a description of contrast and assimilation effects which can be demonstrated in judgments of physical stimuli in the psychological laboratory, as well as in judgments of weaponry.

Deterrence in Small and Large Groups

In the 1949 intergroup relations experiment, one group adopted a strategy to deter the other from future raids on its cabin. They collected green apples "just in case," to be prepared. The other group promptly began collecting apples themselves, and these also were hoarded against eventuality of attack. Although expressly forbidden by the research staff and actually prevented on one occasion, the upper crust of one group succeeded in carrying out a raid when both groups had what they considered ample supplies of apples.

Modern nations are very different from small groups, of course. But their leaders and citizens are human beings whose psychologies are not exempt from processes found in small groups. The Stanford political scientist Robert North and his associates (1963) have demonstrated that policy-makers of five major powers prior to World War I manifested similar tendencies. Making content analyses of political documents and correlated statistical summaries of economic indices, they have shown that all five powers saw themselves as instrumentalities for friendship, but that three also regarded themselves as targets of hostility. Their perceptions of each other and the selection of information that agreed with these self-other images were most consistent during the critical days after Sarajevo, the very time when accurate assessment was most needed.

Today nations have more modern means of detection and assessment of each other's capabilities; but these have not been notably accurate. We need not minimize the importance of powerful interest groups promoting armaments for commercial gain. But their efforts could not succeed without a great margin for error in assessment of defensive and offensive needs. The result is a world in which giant powers possess thermonuclear might sufficient for total annihilation, and several others possess either smaller stores or the potential for their production. To imagine that the use of formal logic or empirical predictions from high-speed computers can put sufficient exactness into risk-taking in such a situation is the rankest science fiction. As noted by one of the early authorities in simulation of international decisions through computers, Oliver Benson (1961), the outcome of a computer analysis is always dependent upon the information and program fed to it by a human being.

The brinkmanship and deterrent strategies of recent years have produced an atmosphere in which the speculations of the strategists are regarded as "scientific." Quite aside from any moral considerations, how is it possible to accept as "scientific" an idle speculation by a strategist about whether the Soviets would be deterred by the loss of two, ten, or fifty of their cities? What is scientific in speculating on whether the United States would lose two or sixty or a hundred million lives in carrying out threats against aggressive action by others (cf. Rappaport, 1964, pp. 106–107)?

Of course, the technicians of deterrence are not solely responsible for turning speculations about the risks of power plays into a pseudo-scientific parlor game. Politicians and scientists also have engaged in it. Some scientists have published estimates on the hazards of fallout, on the damaging power of thermonuclear weapons, and on the capability of current stockpiles for destruction, which are based on the best scientific evidence and are presented with the desire to inform. Such efforts are legitimate

Figure 7.1

Glorification of in-group and derogation of adversary. Two of the Red Devil posters.

Reprinted by permission of Harper & Row, Publishers, from *Groups in Harmony and Tension,* by Muzafer & Carolyn Sherif, 1953.

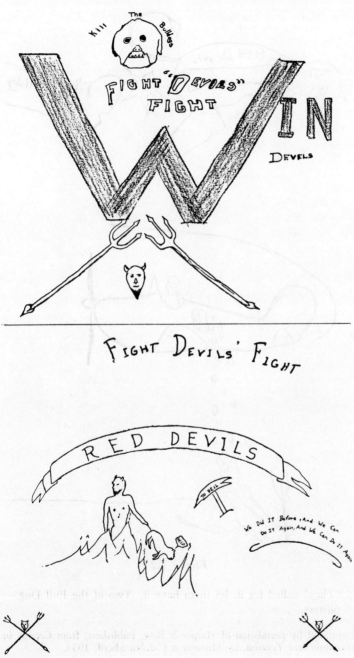

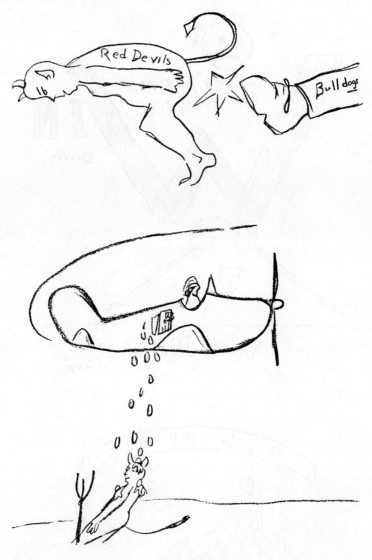

Figure 7.2

"They" called for it, let them have it. Two of the Bull Dog posters.

scientific activities and important contributions to public information. But, in some cases, there appears to be an equally sincere desire to confuse the public, to create a foggy atmosphere in which particular policies may be more easily pursued within the deterrence formula.

A 1959 hearing before Congress produced the estimate that a 3000 megaton attack distributed among seventy-one major cities of the United States would result in over fifty-nine million casualties, of whom only seventeen million would have a chance of surviving (Fowler, 1960, p. 213). In 1961, an account of the power of a 50 megaton explosion directed at New York City was given (Etzioni, 1962, p. 278). It predicted that such a blast and its secondary effects would kill nearly all exposed persons in a forty-nine mile radius. Before President Kennedy's death, he stated that the result of a major "error" in deterrent strategy would result in one hundred and fifty million dead in eighteen hours (cf. Etzioni, 1963).

These estimates reflect two important sources of variation: first, the dependence of any such estimate upon assumptions about the type, power, delivery, and timing of any blow or counterblow which would be made; second, the increasing power, volume, and efficient means of delivering thermonuclear weapons. According to the physicist Teller (1961) the weapons of 1960 were a thousand times more "efficient" than those ten years earlier (p. 34). Hans Bethe (1961, p. 35) reported that "Russia and the United States are fully capable of destroying each other several times over." And Lapp concluded that "stockpiles are more than adequate to spread radioactive lethality over an entire continental land mass" (1960, p. 173).

These are "hard facts," borrowing the phrase from North (1962), of which people should be informed to clear the air of hair-splitting by strategists, scientists, and politicians, or whoever would minimize the threat such stockpiles constitute for the survival of the human race as it is now known. The hair-splitting starts when scientists or technicians begin to assign probabilities and make estimates about the outcomes of deterrent strategies, which have no scientific basis and deserve no more respect than daydreams.

Noting the public confusion about the dangers of fallout, one physicist commented that the Atomic Energy Commission is charged with the responsibility for public assessment of scientific information but "has done little to dispel the confusion. Its public pronouncements seem to have been aimed at reassuring rather than informing" (Fowler, 1960, p. 7). By hazarding guesses about the capabilities and intent of adversaries, the interpretation of scientific evidence becomes support for specific deterrent policies, as when the head of the Atomic Energy Commission flatly denied the dangers of fallout during the 1956 election campaign and completely changed his position three years later.

The physicist who urges the expansion of nuclear arms to include more "tactical weaponry," because they are "less expensive and therefore available in greater numbers," and permit "limited" warfare without "excessive" radioactive contamination, is not functioning as a scientist (Teller, 1961, pp. 44–45). He is proposing military strategy based on the dubious assumption that the parties attacked by the tactical weaponry will restrict war to the specific area intended by the attacker. In this area, a military expert's opinion is more pertinent. General Lauris Norstad, for example, gave this reply when asked by a member of Congress if a limited war with atomic weapons was feasible:

> I do not agree with those people who say you can control the size of this fire, the size of this blast, neatly, cold-bloodedly once it starts. I think it is the most dangerous and disastrous thing in the world. I think you must prevent the thing from starting in the first place because once it starts in a critical area . . . it is more likely than not, in my opinion, to explode into the whole thing, whether we like it or the Russians like it or anybody likes it (Fowler, 1960, p. 184).

Naturally, ordinary people do not easily adopt the notion of annihilation of two or sixty or a hundred and fifty million of their fellows, no matter how antagonistic their feelings toward an enemy. As noted in Chapter 3, this is why the pursuit of a strategy of deterrence requires a massive propaganda campaign to fan the fires of hatred for the "enemy." So successful are such campaigns, formulated in terms of protecting all that is near and dear, that surveys comparing the opinions of the general public with those of selected political leaders find greater agreement on the definition of the "enemy" and the necessity of risking nuclear war among the public than among leaders (cf. Paul and Laulicht, 1963).

The final irony of deterrent strategies is that they themselves produce changes among the peoples who follow them. The strategies affect the ordering of their values, which over time must be assumed to remain roughly the same if the strategy is to work. As seen in our experiments, waging a conflict through force and threat of force changes the ordering of priorities *within* each group, the nature of the relationships among the members, the ideas of who is to be heeded and trusted, and the qualities needed in leadership. With each threat and counterthreat, solidarity within the group heightens and the lone voices crying for the priority of goals once prized are silenced.

The deterrent policies have resulted in the concentration on accumulation of weapons of destruction "for peace" to an extent hitherto unknown, paid for, of course, by taxpayers in every locality. So fantastic is this accumulation of arms for any defensive means that it provoked the following statement from the Secretary of Defense: "It exceeds the extent of my imagination to conceive how these forces might be used and what benefit they would be to our nation" (McNamara, 1963).

Here, then, is the evidence of how accurately a nation may calculate its needs to support a deterrent policy. The errors could be written off as foolish waste, like a woman with too many hats, but that the policy has also given rise to a world of other nations similarly bloated with weapons and of peoples barraged by "information" calculated to make them more willing to support their use.

This setting, dominated by threatened violence and actual violence, has affected, and will further affect, the relative importance assigned to problems of traditional and immediate concern within each country. Problems of work, education, leisure, and cultural development all are affected, and their urgency is altered. The international situation affects the choice of leadership within the countries, the ways human beings spend their lives, the financial arrangements of families, and the viewpoints of youth toward their present and future. The ultimate effect of strategies of mutual deterrence between nations is drastic change in the ways of life, the goals, and the personal outlooks of individuals *within* the nations.

Nonviolent Resistance and the Reduction of Hostility

Deterrence is meaningful only *between* nations or groups (such as bands of brigands) operating apart from external authority. Nonviolent resistance, or noncooperation, on the other hand, is meaningful only when one party to conflict can enforce its will and the other has no forceful means with which to counter.

The doctrine is at least as old as the teachings of Jesus, who counselled "love thine enemy" and "turn the other cheek" to displays of violence. It was Gandhi in colonial India who developed nonviolent noncooperation as a means of "pitting of one's whole soul against the will of the tyrant" (Nehru, 1961, p. 82, quoting Gandhi, 1920). Both Gandhi and subsequent leaders of nonviolent movements (e.g., King 1958) have recognized nonviolence as a policy for waging conflict by those with no forceful means available.

Nonviolent resistance needs no detailed explanation as a method of struggle under dire circumstances. Both history and current events show that, for a solidary group, it is an effective policy under the circumstances described, which include a suppressed population of sufficient number to make its noncooperation or nonviolent resistance felt. It is also abundantly clear from actual events that nonviolent strategies in situations of any import require human courage and heroism of the highest order ever invoked by proponents of violence — a point on which Gandhi had to proselytize to guard his male followers from charges of cowardice and "unmanliness."

In fact, the nonviolent movements have clarified the sources of human bravery and courage, those admirable qualities displayed by exceptional individuals in times of stress. The psychiatrist Jerome Frank (1964) has indicated the importance of adherence to group standards in individual acts of courage by noting the various forms human bravery has taken:

> . . . the nonviolent campaigns led by Gandhi in India and King in the United States . . . both succeeded in creating group standards which divorced courage from violence. Refusal to resort to violence became the sign of firmness of will: resort to violence was a sign of cowardice (p. 46).

Here, our interest is in the implications of nonviolent strategies for reduction of conflict and hostility. The key to this problem, as cogently noted by Jerome Frank (1963), lies in the after-effects of the conflict. The results of violence are well documented: human tragedy, mutual attribution of blame for it, rancor and bitterness. Frank has suggested reasons why nonviolent strategies in conflict provide a more congenial basis for the negotiations that must accompany the reduction of conflict and hostility.

The effectiveness of nonviolent methods does not lie solely in the inconveniencing of the opponent — the crowding of his jails or the use of his resources. Rather, writes Frank, it lies in the violation of some central and major value of the aggressor as a result of his *own behavior* toward the subordinate group. In the case of the boycott, the injury is monetary, of course. But if the enforcer and the victim share certain common values, such as belief in equal justice, the nonviolent strategy in effect forces the enforcer to violate these values. To the extent that enforcer and victim share common values, feelings of guilt in the aggressor are aroused by the nonviolent technique. Thus, the effective nonviolent strategy contains its own seeds for conciliation under these circumstances.

Certainly the absence of physical injury to the opponent by the nonviolent resister reduces the residue of mutual hurt that ordinarily impedes efforts to reduce conflict, provided, of course, that the resister can suppress his own memory of being oppressed. The atmosphere for transaction and negotiations to settle differences after a successful nonviolent movement probably differs from that in which both parties were aggressively violent. However, there is no evidence as yet that the problems of intergroup hostility disappear following successful conduct of nonviolent resistance, any more than they do following the cessation of open conflict conducted by other means.

In the next chapter, we turn to measures that do hold promise in reducing conflict and hostility.

8

Measures That Can Reduce Intergroup Conflict

In this chapter, we turn to measures intended to contribute to the reduction of intergroup tensions within countries and the easing of suspicious animosities between nations. Our particular interest will be the conditions necessary for realizing their potential.

The measures to be discussed are positive, and they are not mutually exclusive. In fact, any single measure will be more effective if coordinated with others.

For example, legislation such as the Civil Rights Act of 1964 has the potential to reduce conflicts by setting definite bounds and outlawing various discriminatory practices in certain public areas of behavior. Clearly, compliance with the law will be more widespread, accompanied by less strife, and accelerated if there is a "change of heart" in the islands of resistance through dissemination of correct information, contact among Negroes and whites in other contexts, and give-and-take between their leaders on community and regional levels. The point needs no elaboration since it is obvious that none of these measures singly, nor the mere passage of a law, will produce the intended results.

Similarly, on an international level, the program for "Graduated Reciprocation in Tension-reduction" (GRIT) proposed by an outstanding American psychologist, Charles Osgood (1962), presupposes the use of a variety of measures. The plan is concerned with turning the tide of international rancor and reversing the upward spiral of the arms race, with its staggering potential of destruction.

Osgood proposes that one of the giants in the arms race initiate a step-by-step reversal of the spiral "through a carefully planned and executed unilateral peace offensive to invite reciprocation" from the opposite bloc. He proposes that unilateral initiative, clearly proclaimed well in advance of execution and representing a sincere intent to reduce intergroup tension, will be conducive to similar steps on the part of others toward reversing the horrifying spiral of armaments (see especially 1962, pp. 98–108). The plan is highly imaginative and the description of the contemporary international scene with its particular stereotypic mentality is instructive.

The complexities of legislation providing sanctions, law enforcement, and the political and economic steps required to reverse the arms race are beyond the scope of this book and the author's ken. We do not feel qualified from a technical point of view to evaluate specific legislation proposed or specific actions in international relations. However, our discussion of the conditions in which information, negotiations by leaders, and contacts between individuals belonging to different groups can be effective does have bearing on compliance to legislation and on problems bound to be encountered in attempts to reverse the arms spiral. What follows, then, is an analysis of the conditions under which intergroup communication can be utilized effectively for genuine reduction of intergroup hostility. The analysis is equally applicable in regard to compliance to legislation and to practical plans to secure international peace.

THE MOTIVATIONAL BASE FOR EFFECTIVE MEASURES

The formulations and the pointers from research findings in this book require that certain questions be posed about measures proposed for reduction of intergroup hostilities. *Under what conditions* is dissemination of accurate information effective in changing discriminatory or antagonistic attitudes? *Under what conditions* can leaders of mutually hostile groups take bold, imaginative steps toward resolving their differences without being torn from their positions of effective power by their own people? *Under what conditions* are face-to-face contacts among people from antagonistic groups conducive to development of mutual trust and respect? As everyone knows, contacts among antagonists and their spokesmen are often used for gaining propaganda advantage or for other vested interests.

On the basis of research, we conclude that these measurse can be effective, singly or in combination, when there is initially a motivational base encompassing members of all groups caught in conflict. Such a motivational base is provided when the conflicting groups and their respective members are directed towards superordinate goals, clearly perceived and requiring joint efforts for attainment.

A superordinate goal cannot be fabricated through the manipulative devices of one group. In the present state of dependence of group upon group and nation upon nation, there already are compelling superordinate goals, awaiting accentuation by every group. If feelings of urgency are to be aroused among people living in more or less "closed" settings, the fog of complexities surrounding these goals must be lifted. They must be made concrete across distances and other barriers.

When groups are caught in conflict, superordinate goals to which all are directed provide the motivational base essential if specific measures are to be effective. Therefore, superordinate goals should not be regarded as one of several alternative measures that may reduce intergroup conflict. They provide the essential condition for the ultimate effectiveness of any measure to be discussed in this chapter.

But now let us scrutinize the effectiveness of specific measures in the light of research findings. The specific measures to be considered are: the dissemination of information; conferences of leaders and representatives; and programs providing opportunity for face-to-face contact among individuals belonging to different groups.

DISSEMINATION OF INFORMATION

Obviously, dissemination of information is necessary for changes in hostile intergroup relations and attitudes. Information campaigns are intended to change attitudes of hatred and supremacy on the part of antagonistic groups to mutual liking and recognition of each other's human dignity.

Of course, hatred, desire to dominate, and evil designs *can* be altered by acceptance of valid information and recognition of the futility of friction. People are perfectly capable of seeing the reasonableness of harmony over strife and of good will over bigotry, *if* they are willing to expose themselves to and assimilate correct information. Then, what stands in the way? Why are proclamations of human rights and pronouncements from scientific, humanistic, and religious sources presenting scientific and moral bases for good will and peace on earth of so little avail? Why do campaigns disseminating accurate information so frequently fail?

Research on attitudes and attitude change is instructive. Here, we can present only the main generalizations from a vast body of findings (cf. Klapper, 1960; Hovland, 1959; Sherif, Sherif, and Nebergall, 1965). Some of these generalizations were summarized in Chapter 2 in the discussion of categorical thinking and the substantive mentality. Others were included in Chapter 5, in connection with the experiments on the rise of unfavorable attitudes and their effects on the way "facts" are subsequently perceived.

Let us start by considering the fact that all our reception of incoming information is necessarily *selective*. None of us can attend to more than a fraction of what is available to us. However, psychological selectivity is systematically biased by a spontaneous screening process wrought through the kind of a person we have become. Our receptivity for information is narrowed to what is relevant and fits readily into our ongoing interests, to the bounds of what we already consider acceptable, and what we expect on the basis of our established attitudes.

In addition, there is an external screening process through the family, church, school, government, and other agencies that has a great influence on what we are exposed to. The selectors of information, events, and items of entertainment to be presented on the mass media are a signfiicant part of this screening process. Their selectivity follows the same laws; it too is governed by personal interests, premises, and commitments. "All the news that is fit to print" is all the news filtered through the selectivity of certain people who are in the position to select what is printed. Their selectivity, too, affects the way in which information is presented — whether it is placed in screaming headlines or buried in small print beside a vivid advertisement.

Role of Attitude in Reacting to Communication

Of concern to us here is the news item, lecture, discussion, or dramatization concerning an intergroup event or problem. The individual is exposed to it in a face-to-face situation or through mass communication. What a person is exposed to depends upon both the selectors of information and upon his own attention. His decision to receive the information or not to receive it is guided by his interests and attitudes, as is his reaction to the communication once he listens and watches. Interpretation of the information, the person's conception of the position it presents, and his evaluation of it are governed by his own stand on the issue at hand or toward the group which is the topic of communication (Sherif and Hovland, 1961; Sherif, Sherif, and Nebergall, 1965).

The communication dealing with a controversial social issue or with a friendly group or a detested group is not received by an empty black box. Its reception is not like the television screen that projects the same image on all sets, with slight variations.

The human mind is an active and transforming instrument. Once exposed to a communication, it filters the information, comparing it to its existing store and seeking to categorize the incoming messages relative to that existing store. Because of this comparison process, the information dealing with a human group or a controversial issue is not categorized in the same way by different persons.

In reacting to a communication about another human group or a controversial issue, we use as a basis for comparison the "facts" we hold true and acceptable. Usually these are "facts" we have learned from those most respected and significant in our lives, who are as a rule in our own reference groups. If the communication's position is not too distant from our own standard "facts," we locate it closer to our position than it is. This tendency to pull a position closer to our own and embrace it within our existing scheme of acceptable information is called an "assimilation effect." The range of information we use as the standard for comparison is referred to as the "latitude of acceptance."

When a person embraces a position advocated in communication by assimilating it toward his latitude of acceptance, there are affective and emotional consequences. The information is appraised as "true" and "factual," "nonpropagandistic" and "fair." It is more congenial than information about issues or groups about which the person is impartial, noncommittal, or uninformed.

On the other hand, if the communication presents information supporting a position running considerably counter to our own stand on the matter, we locate it further away from our own standard than it is. This exaggeration of difference is called a "contrast effect." It occurs when the communication falls near or within the range of information we reject, that is, the "latitude of rejection."

The contrast effect is associated with affective-emotional consequences. The information presented in communication is categorized as "false" and "propagandistic." It is irritating and even obnoxious. Even if the source is unknown, it is treated as the handiwork of the wicked or the crackpot, lacking a human sense of proportion and reason.

Compared to what the person already cherishes as true and acceptable, the discrepant information is considered nonsense or an outrage to be dumped into the bin of all that is detestable in his scheme of things — his latitude of rejection. Thus, even a communication moderately opposed to his stand is seen as extreme and radical. Needless to say, this perception is associated with a sense of being victimized by propaganda.

Quite logically, the individual is impervious to information designed to change his attitude on an issue in directions that are, to him, unreasonable nonsense. The result is irritation at being exposed to such a propaganda device, even though the message contains objectively correct information and the conclusions are based on scientific research on the social or national issue.

The end-products of this psychological process were reported in discussing group stereotypes (Chapter 2) and the vicious circle of "who is to blame" in assessing the etiology of intergroup frictions (Chapter 7). A specific message is considered as *education* when it falls within or near the latitude of acceptance established on an issue within our reference groups. The same message is dubbed *propaganda* if it falls near or within the vast dumping ground of our latitude of rejection. We have different words for actions and events in these two ranges. Death inflicted in our cause is heroic, but the same act committed by our enemy is murder.

We must stress that these limitations in the reception of information are not illogical or irrational, given the standards an individual uses in appraising it. He does not experience contradiction, a sense of guilt, or shame in making such harsh evaluations of objective information because, given his premises, he is making an objective judgment. He is not aware of the distortions that actually occur in his placement of the information. If he is a member of an in-group to which he is deeply loyal, the standards of that group are his standards in appraising incoming information. Persons with the opposed view displace information in the opposite direction.

This description of the psychological process in the reception and evaluation of information by members of a closed group or society is not an attempt to justify either the process or the group. We do not want to imply that all individuals or all groups are so closed that their standards for assessing incoming information are narrow and rigid. However, as we have seen, one effect of intergroup conflict is to standardize and solidify the bounds of what is acceptable and what is not.

The evaluation scheme of people committed to a "closed society" is presented to them as absolute and impervious to the consequences of larger systems. We have discussed such schemes because the target populations for information disseminated to reduce intergroup hostility are often members of "closed societies." Those who have a broader perspective for evaluating information in terms of its scientific basis are not the serious targets for such campaigns. They are likely to seek out information that is scientifically based, even if it is difficult to obtain.

The implications of this analysis can be expressed briefly. Scientific information about the basic humanity of all groups will fall on deaf ears unless prevailing doctrines of closed groups and closed societies become permeable. The antidote is not more information for more deaf ears. The antidote must lie in concrete events and active moves to demonstrate to various groups that they, too, are functionally related to others. Interdependent ties among groups cannot be formalized in effective organizational arrangements until this becomes clear to them.

Probably most important in the modern world is the promotion in all groups of a keen awareness of the present state of technology, including weapons of destruction. In this area, all the great nations share a common predicament that inevitably will affect the destinies of other nations, and groups within them. This realization in turn provides effective ground for recognition of a superordinate goal shared by all human groupings — survival of human beings, along with all that is precious in the painfully accumulated cultures of all peoples.

POLICY DECISIONS AND NEGOTIATIONS
OF LEADERS

Whatever confrontations the rank and file of antagonistic groups may have, the decisive encounters in intergroup disputes are, sooner or later, confrontations of their respective spokesmen. Apart from very small neighborhood groups, human groups express their gripes, demands, agreements, disagreements, and protests through spokesmen.

The spokesman of a group, small or large, may be its elected or acknowledged leader, or his delegate. If the prevailing transfer of power is hereditary, the leader may be the hereditary chief or king. More usually, today, he is selected by some means to represent his people in intergroup encounters.

Only the acknowledged leaders of groups can commit their people to a policy, be it in the direction of conflict or of peace. The policy entertained and negotiations conducted by leaders of groups in conflict, or by representatives endowed with their power, can be highly effective in resolving intergroup disputes. However, their effectiveness is limited by the fact that the power of a leader and his delegates is not absolute. It cannot insure always the full-hearted, or even the effective commitment of his people to the policy adopted, whether this be a "hard line" or "soft line" toward the antagonist. The leader's power in the cozy or heated atmosphere of the negotiations is very great, but it cannot always insure support for his decision, a joint proclamation, treaty, or agreement on peace or war.

Under what conditions can a leader or his delegates commit his people in a specific direction? We shall restrict the discussion to modern human groupings whose leaders claim to represent the interests of their people or owe their leadership to their people's consent and/or willing support.

The Power of Leadership
and Its Bounds

The conception of what leaders can and cannot accomplish in intergroup negotiations is heavily colored by traditional views of leadership. The traditional conception assumed a sharp dichotomy between the leader and his group, with the leader the repository of unlimited power and superior talents in a universe of his own, while his group exists in an entirely different universe. In their little world, the rank and file respond to signals for feeling and action emanating from the leader's universe, which is splendidly isolated from their own. To accentuate our point, we have deliberately overdrawn this relic dichotomy between the leader and his people.

The groundwork of the present discussion was laid in Chapter 1, where leadership, representation, and negotiation were characterized as integral aspects of group functioning. The leader of a group is *part* of the group, not outside it, despite the fact that he wields the greatest power over the rest.

Being an integral part of the group, the leader himself is not immune to the corrective sanctions applied to any member who steps out of the acceptable bounds of outlook and the developing trends in his group, vis à vis the adversary. In some matters, he has more leeway than members with less power, but it is precisely in the most crucial issues that he must be exemplary of the group's values and stay within their narrow bounds (cf. Sherif and Sherif, 1964). Even if he was more influential than others in creating the prevailing mood for dealing with an adversary, he has to stick to that prevailing mood. Especially in times of crisis, of imminent or actual flareups between groups, the leader has to be the front line in resolute rejection of the adversary (cf. Gouldner, 1954).

If the prevailing trend between groups is friendly, the leader must be exemplary in typifying friendship. If the trend is toward active conflict, he has to be exemplary in devising ways and means to inflict destruction on the enemy. Even if he were the most active in promoting the trend toward conflict, the growth of a widespread image of him as "soft" on the adversary or appeasing in his demands may shatter his effectiveness as a leader. Ultimately, it may result in his downfall.

These facts have been demonstrated time and again by faltering leaders in intergroup crises. They are perfectly understandable in the light of research on the characteristics of effective leaders who retain the backing of their people. Evidence shows that the stuff of which leaders are made is not a unitary personal quality generated in the breast of the leader. The qualities that distinguish a leader from the rest of the people within his fold and that give him the edge over other aspirants are those pertinent to the exigencies of the situations and the challenges of problems facing the group.

The qualities that promote a particular person as a leader are best expressed as *interactional between the leader and his people within the context of the urgent problems of situations at hand.* For example, we cannot dismiss lightly the contention that Winston Churchill's political life might have been at an end, despite his extraordinary personal characteristics, if Britain's situation of 1940 had not called for a leader with dramatic personal qualities, completely mobilized and singlemindedly fixated on victory.

The interactional nature of the emergence of a leader and of his effectiveness is well summarized by Cecil Gibb, who gave one of the most comprehensive and insightful surveys of leadership studies as of 1954:

Leadership is an interactional phenomenon, and interaction theory seems best fitted to provide a framework for studies of leadership. The emergence of group structure and the differentiation of function of group members depend upon the interaction of those members, and are general group phenomena. An individual's assumption of the leader role depends not only upon the role needs of the group and upon his individual attributes of personality, but also upon the members' perception of him as filling the group role requirements. These, in turn, vary as the situation and the task alter. In general, it may be said that leadership is a function of personality and of the social situation and of these two in interaction (1954, p. 917).

Gibb's conclusion is very much in line with the generalizations reached by Stogdill (1948) in his careful critical survey of personal factors associated with leadership and his research program since then on leadership in large organizations. The constant interaction between a leader and his group within the framework of binding expectations and prevailing trends in the group is a major influence in intergroup confrontations, especially in times of crisis. In times of crisis, loyalty and exemplary opposition to the adversary are at a high premium for all. Then, the demands on the leader for forceful expression of his unflinching opposition to the adversary are particularly exacting. *His choice of alternative measures is restricted far more than the range of alternatives that may be logical, well calculated, and feasible in more normal times.*

This conclusion is illustrated by the "peace mission" of a high status member at the height of intergroup conflict in one of our experiments. An individual holding a high position in his own group decided, with the best of motives, that the time had come to negotiate peaceful relations with the hostile group. He was received by them as an enemy who sought to mislead them with pretended expressions of reconciliation. His departure was accompanied by a hail of "ammunition," in this case, green apples, collected by the group "in case" they were attacked. Equally interesting was the fate of this individual when he returned to his own group. Far from being received as a hero, he was chastised for even making the attempt.

This is but one of many examples that leadership, representation, and negotiation between groups are governed according to bounds acceptable in each group. If he is to negotiate effectively, a leader or his delegate must remain a part of his group. In order to do so, he must act in ways his fellow members regard as acceptable and decent, in terms of their group's definitions.

The realistic alternatives a leader or negotiator can consider, therefore, are limited. Not all possible alternatives that are logically conceivable are realistically available to him. The realistic alternatives are those within or near the bounds of acceptability to members of his own group at the time. In large groups, where negotiations may be conducted in secret, a leader has somewhat more latitude. But there is not one leader in the world today who could long remain in power after committing his group to a course clearly unacceptable to the members.

For example, everyone is familiar with the tragic fate of President Woodrow Wilson who, even as twice-elected president, could not commit his own country to participation in the League of Nations to whose very creation he had sacrificed so much devotion and effort. Effective leaders are guided by such lessons from their predecessors. Even those whose power is so great that their opponents dub them "dictators" make commitments to other groups only after "preparing the ground" within the power structure of their own people.

The necessity of "preparing the ground" before taking steps toward expanding intergroup commitments was well illustrated in the response of President Franklin D. Roosevelt to the proposal by his Secretary of Labor, Frances Perkins, that the United States join the International Labor Organization:

> He thought a minute and said, "Yes, certainly, *but* remember a few things. Don't try to do this without the full assent and understanding of the members of Congress primarily responsible for foreign policy . . . Remember how Wilson lost the League of Nations . . . lost the opportunity for the United States to take part in the most important international undertaking ever conceived. He lost it by not getting Congress to participate. They have a sense of responsibility, and they can't have sincere convictions unless they are given a chance to examine the situation at close range. Make sure that the men on the Senate Foreign Relations Committee have information and convictions about this idea of our going into the ILO . . . You know we stayed out of the ILO only because there was such terrible opposition to the League of Nations." He advised

me . . . not to let the old prejudice be an obstacle to this one small aspect of international cooperation . . . "I may be the President of the United States, I may be in favor of the ILO, but I can't do it alone . . . and you must prepare the way systematically and carefully. Take plenty of time about it. Don't be discouraged. Give them ample opportunity to examine all the facts" (1946, p. 340).

Thus, one leader revealed his awareness that leadership is a product of give-and-take between the leader and his group, as concluded by Gibb. Another example is given by Marshall Montgomery, who spent some days as a house guest of Nehru in preparation for his book *The Path to Leadership* (1961). Nehru, one of the leaders beloved by his people, conceived of leadership in the following terms, as reported by Montgomery:

> He [Nehru] himself is fully aware of this power, and of the problems it creates. In our talks he emphasized the point constantly that *a leader cannot act to a degree beyond* what the people will take; he must, of course, have courage, but if the people will not follow his decisions he will inevitably fall (p. 90; italics in original).

Some "Built-in" Limitations on Leadership of Modern Nations

The leader of a modern nation is limited by certain practices which pervade the process of in-group functioning and intergroup negotiation. One is the hard-to-cure procedure within groups of dealing with intergroup tension through deciding "who's to blame." This practice invariably produces a vicious circle of accusation and counteraccusation between groups that intensifies intergroup hatred (see Chapter 7). In the past, this vicious circle has resulted in building images of the adversary as a monster beyond the pale of humanity, and an image of the in-group as self-righteous and just.

Equally restricting for leaders is the wide credence given to a "balance of power" formula, now groomed for respectability with its new label "deterrence." Hired technicians working within the narrow domain of their specialties adorn the formula with jargon derived from mathematical and economic models, technically sophisticated but sadly lacking in valid assumptions about the behavior of human beings. As analyzed in the last chapter, the formula can only contribute to heightening the arms race spiral.

The efforts of the technicians to use awe-inspiring models and computer simulation to disguise the poverty and deathly countenance of their "balance of power" formula are not to be judged sheerly on moral grounds; their own pretense is "rationality" and "science," which cannot countenance edifices built on erroneous assumptions.

A rose by any other name smells as sweet, and deterrence smells of preparation for war, which the balance of power formula has always been. Elegant trappings of mathematical theory and the frenzied click of high speed computers do not change the odor of powder, ruined cities, and death. For despite the progress made by the most advanced thinkers in political science, communication, and military strategy, there is no guarantee that the precautions and checks against hasty reaction to threat will prevent confrontations of global proportions with weapons whose staggering might makes the last World War seem like a tribal engagement.

No leader, no matter how powerful, can guarantee that worldwide conflagration on a truly modern scale will not occur if the present practices of assigning blame and relying on deterrence are continued. Sooner or later, he will find himself in a situation in which things are out of hand, owing to a slight miscalculation of someone somewhere, or a slight overreaction by one link in the elaborate chain created by these practices.

We are told by those in select circles who have the details of knowhow that a deadly showdown between giant blocs of nations will mean mortal destruction to all in its wake, leaving a world hardly recognizable, probably not habitable. A deadly showdown, we are told by the creators of weapons whose power is measured in megatons, will bring down the vanquished and victor, engulfing all persons on each side in a world completely unknown to modern sophisticated man. Even those now making a valiant effort to stay noncommitted to one or another giant bloc of nations will not be spared.

There is one superordinate goal for all peoples in all places that leaders can cultivate within the bounds of any human system of living. It is the goal of human survival. Human beings in the East and West alike will awaken as they become aware of the all-pervasive shadow over their future. The shadow holds a predicament for all human beings. But, beyond the fear, there can be awakened the stupendous superordinate goal of existing as human beings alive on the face of an earth which can provide for their needs, as contrasted with a creature sealed underground for weeks against the immediate hazards of radiation poisoning — torn from

human moorings — who can emerge only to a world so despoiled
as to destroy him and his survivors or to provide a living hell.

To human beings, survival as an animal pitifully adapted to
unheard-of surroundings has never been a goal. Survival as human
beings of diverse conceptions about life in diverse environments is
a goal. To humans, *living* includes all that has been painfully built
through centuries and is precious as their cultural heritage.

The role of leadership in this distinctly modern situation should
be clear: to prepare and cultivate the ground within their groups
toward human survival. Yet, there are islands of influential groups
in various places living in a fool's paradise. They are still captivated
by the image of themselves in their self-contained gardens. They
see others in terms of categorical images arranged along superiority
lines inherited from the past. They crusade for policies based on
such obsolete arrangements, obsolete because any presumed "scientific" basis disappeared before it was established and actualities are
now defying it. They crusade for measures that foster the flareup
of old prejudices and hatreds, oblivious of the fact that showdowns
today are homicidal. Their old notions of contained struggles, now
called "limited war," ignore the facts of changing power relations.
Limited wars in the past depended on tacit agreements among
established powers to contain conflict.

Leaders of modern nations have less and less choice among
diverse alternatives. They have a choice, on the one hand, between
attempting to use their power to inform their people about the
realities of modern technology that increase man's dependence on
man and, on the other hand, of remaining within the grooves
already established and acceptable within their group. The first
alternative is creative, but it requires the leaders' determined efforts
to prepare the ground for re-orientation toward the superordinate
goal of human survival.

Preparing the ground so that leaders can take bolder and imaginative steps toward the superordinate goal of survival involves
sharing with their people exactly what is at stake in concrete terms
they can understand. If people everywhere will fully realize,
through vivid picture, concrete illustration, and simple words, the
grim consequences of a deadly showdown, they will not quibble
over the fantastic disagreements among strategists as to whether
the exact figure of dead will be two or ten or sixty or one hundred
and sixty million.

Once people share this information fully, leaders caught in
prevailing intergroup disputes will feel safer in taking the bold and
imaginative steps that are needed, in concert with their opposite

numbers. Desperate cries for unilateral action toward aggression and for reconciliation will become events of historical interest, for aggression will be out of bounds for the groups in question and efforts toward reconciliation will bring responses now only to be devoutly wished.

Preparing such ground requires from leaders more than making decisions and entering agreements *for* their people. It requires leaders to see that people are informed about the decision-making and about the means they have at their disposal to implement decisions. It requires launching multimillion dollar programs, not unilaterally, but in earnest agreement with all parties to intergroup conflict. Those who object to programs of these proportions may well ponder on the predicament produced by programs of similar cost whose only benefit is destruction, and which, if ever followed to their logical conclusion, offer no opportunity for backtracking.

How can leaders accomplish this groundwork? The details of the grim consequences of pursuing armed conflict in the modern world should be frequent topics at meetings of parents, of teachers, of writers. Education in the modern world should include as an integral part the realities of modern arms and the means of transporting them. These realities are obscured when scientists quibble over the exact number in millions of dead. To people not befogged by the strategic thinking, the lower, median, or upper limit of estimates by scientists are equally overwhelming. The point is not the precise number, but that human life is being discussed and that the despoiling of the earthly environment for those who do survive is thereby implied.

This book is not the place for blueprints on how a leader can prepare the ground. Leaders will have to show their acumen in working out blueprints in economic, political, or military spheres. But if there are leaders who want to make history, the one sure step they can take away from holocaust, toward the human future, is to alert their peoples to whatever superordinate goals exist among men.

FACE-TO-FACE RELATIONSHIPS, EXCHANGE OF PERSONS, AND OTHER CONTACT SITUATIONS

Intergroup dealings require transactions between members of the respective groups, whether they are friendly or unfriendly, trustful or distrustful. Social units caught within the same intergroup system cannot avoid each other entirely. Their dealings are carried out through communication and face-to-face contacts between individual members of the respective groups. In the long run, the heightening of conflict and its reduction are translated into words and actions during face-to-face encounters between some members of the groups.

So there is no question that contact between groups is necessary for any change in their relationships. Here, our concern is with contact between members of different groups in pleasant social contexts. Is the pleasantness of a social context in which diverse peoples meet as host and guest, or as equals, a sufficient condition for the reduction of existing hostility between them? Are social hours of coffee-sipping in cozy surroundings, joint entertainments, joint instruction, dancing together on special occasions, or living together in one house sufficient to bring about harmony between persons belonging to different groups?

An Illustrative Study

One form of intergroup contact intended to promote friendship is exchange of persons, including students. In line with the indications of other studies, our recent research shows that a sojourn as a student in the United States does have an impact on the attitudes of the visitor. However, the direction of the impact depends on the visitor's reference groups (Russell and Sherif, 1966).

In our recent research on Asian and South American students in the United States, we found that some of the students had shifted their reference groups from the country of origin to the United States, the proportions varying for students of different nationalities but exceeding 50 per cent in some cases. When these students, who had taken the United States as their reference group, assessed the importance of various issues they faced as students and issues that faced the United States, their appraisals were closely similar to United States students taking the same academic course of study.

Still other students revealed weakened ties with their home country, but lacked a single national reference group. They indicated equal preference for several countries other than their own, almost always Western European countries and the United States. Their appraisals differed more from the matched United States students. However, having no single reference country, their reactions were heterogeneous, differing considerably among themselves.

The foreign students whose appraisals of the United States differed most from those of native United States students and from the acculturated foreign students mentioned above were those with strong identifications with their home country. Dedication to home country was associated with many contrasting appraisals of the importance of problems facing the United States which, in turn, were quite different from their assessments of problems facing their home country. For example, they saw the problem of minority groups as more important for the United States than did United States students, but regarded this problem of minor importance for their home countries. Unlike United States students, they viewed United States participation in world affairs as a major problem affecting their own country (students from some countries desiring more United States participation in their part of the world and some desiring less).

The differing national reference of foreign students from the same country was, in turn, associated with differences in their informal associations on the campus. Those who had informal reference groups composed of fellow nationals agreed significantly more in their appraisals than those without such ties. The greatest similarity in views of the host country was found among persons participating with like-minded friends in informal groupings. Whether their views were favorable to the host country or not depended upon the strength of their home country identification. In short, contacts with the United States had different impacts, depending in part upon association with like-minded friends who were dedicated to the home country or in the process of shifting to the United States as the primary national identification.

Contact under What Conditions?

It is well known that contact may breed contempt as well as friendship. It will be recalled that in our experiments contact situations designed to bring together antagonistic groups as equals during sumptuous meals and entertainments did not reduce their antagonisms. On the contrary, the contact situations were utilized as occasions to exchange invectives, and degenerated beyond the point of reciprocal attribution of blame for existing tension. They, in turn, became standard occasions for what came to be called "garbage wars." Each group blamed the initial aggressive step on its antagonist. The physical engagement was such a spontaneous flareup, following the exchange of invective and blame-casting, that even the researchers on the spot could not pinpoint the initial aggressor.

When can interaction among members of hostile groups be effective in reducing hostilities? It can be effective when the particular characteristics distinguishing intergroup behavior from other behavior are duly recognized, as stated in Chapter 1. Again, we must ask the question: "Under what conditions?" The naive notion that sheer contiguity under pleasant conditions promotes harmony is sadly disproven.

We may learn something about the answer by considering cases in which contacts fall short of effectiveness. The case of a segregationist is instructive, as presented by Robert Penn Warren in a work incisive both in style and in its analysis of the inner conflict experienced by many a Southerner (Warren, 1956). The segregationist in question already feels, under the impact of events, that something has to be done to give a fair deal to the Negro. He considers the possibility of gestures of "graciousness":

> "Sure, some of us, a lot of us, could manage some graciousness to individual Negroes, some of us were grateful to individuals for being gracious to us. But you know, we couldn't manage it for the race." He thinks a moment, then says: "There is a Negro woman buried in the family burial place. We loved her" (p. 56).

It is a peculiar property of intergroup contacts that the role of one person vis à vis another is not determined solely by personal qualities, nor even by social prescriptions about roles that cut across group lines, such as occupational or educational functions. The salient factor is the standing of the two groups.

Are the individuals participating as equals in this respect, or as superior-inferior, or as rivals? Once this question is answered, there is still the problem of how the contact situation is related to the other spheres of living that absorb the individuals ordinarily. Is the situation an unusual exception, planned under well-meaning patronage but unrelated to the problems that occupy the participants in their day-to-day activities or in their aspirations? What did the participants have to do with arranging the situation? Was it arranged *for* them, without involving them, or was it arranged *by* them? Is there any embracing purpose to the contact, or any continuity between episode after episode of intergroup contact?

Such questions quickly help us differentiate the ineffective from the effective contact situations. In general terms, the effectiveness of contact depends upon the particular group and intergroup framework within which it occurs.

If it were otherwise, we should be sorely tried to explain in any sensible terms why many youngsters who were brought up under the tender care of Negro "mammies" take a segregationist position when grown up. Margaret Long, a writer with extensive first-hand experience in Negro-white interpersonal relations, reported her interviews with young university students in Oxford, Mississippi, shortly after the sobering events of the fall of 1963 (Long, 1963). One of those interviewed was a pleasant and attractive young man who had had a fortunate and pleasant childhood. He described in warm terms the kind associations he had enjoyed with the many Negroes and the children working on his family's estate, one of the oldest in Mississippi. Did these pleasant human associations have any bearing on his conceptions of Negro-white relations? The intergroup demarcations he saw were along superiority-inferiority lines drawn by his family tradition, of which this personable and able young man was most proud. The young man himself put his personal associations with Negroes in the "proper" perspective:

> "Yes, of course I used to play with Negro children. . . . We quit, well, we quit when . . . we both realized the difference, and they went their way and I went mine. . . I feel as do most of the white population of the South that the Negro is inherently unequal . . ." (p. 114).

The indiscriminate assessment of the importance of contact seems to stem from two notions. One is that real accomplishment in getting acquainted and conducting negotiations occurs in pleasant and social surroundings. This notion is doubtless based on the fact that *within* social units such occasions provide opportunity for relaxation and fellowship otherwise hindered by the normal routines of living. The second seems to be the uncritical acceptance of a hedonistic associationism: people like whatever is associated with their pleasures. Both notions are so incomplete as to distort the real importance of contacts in intergroup relations.

Only when erstwhile rivals come into contact in pursuit of a vital purpose that grips all participants can contact situations furnish opportunity for creative moves toward reducing intergroup hostility. The participants must feel a common, steadfast pull in the same direction, if not toward the same actions. Otherwise, contact degenerates into formalistic ritual or into the vicious circle of "who is to blame." Without some interdependence among the parties in contact, face-to-face situations produce lowered thresholds for the verdict of "What else would you expect from such a __ __ __ __?" Without such overriding concerns, petty interpersonal rivalries over financial gain, status advantage, or even over sexual conquest are cast in the scheme of intergroup conflict. Contact is an effective medium for change when groups are directed toward superordinate goals overriding their separate concerns.

What Are the Effective Alternatives?

Several conclusions may be drawn from the discussion of measures to cope with intergroup disputes in these last two chapters. The practices of the past seem "natural," despite their obvious failures, because they are based on unpremeditated assumptions about human behavior and follow the patterns of impulses instigated in intergroup conflict. However, the practice of deciding "who is to blame," with its invariable justification of ourselves and derogation of the opponent, has intensified self-righteousness and hostile attitudes toward others. The pitting of power against power to deter a rival through exceeding or equalizing his might has, sooner or later, always become the harbinger of ruin.

Dissemination of information, negotiation by leaders, and contacts between parties in conflict can be utilized to seek more creative alternatives. Specific adjustments in intergroup relations, such as unilateral display of good will and declarations of peaceful intentions accompanied by concrete evidence of those intentions (for example, reducing one's arsenal), can be beneficial. But for these measures to be effective, singly or in combination, there must be a motivational base common to all parties in conflict. Such a motivational base is provided by superordinate goals.

Superordinate goals cannot be fabricated or unilaterally proposed. They arise in the functional relations between groups, and their possibilities increase with the diversity and volume of concerns affecting both groups. With increased contact and a growing diversity of concerns affecting both sides, each group in an intergroup system becomes more dependent upon the other, so that what happens *within* its bounds is increasingly conditioned by its relations with the other groups in the system.

Such mutual dependence, even though it may be decried within each group, furnishes fertile soil for common predicaments. The predicament of one group becomes a predicament to other groups in the system. Thus, the attainment of compelling goals to which all aspire becomes contingent upon all parties pulling together in the same direction.

Superordinate goals are not "devices" to be manipulated in dealing with intergroup tensions. They must arise from the relationships between groups in a fashion so compelling that they can be recognized within each group. This is the source of a motivational compulsion cutting across the diversity of hopes and ambitions in different groups. With such a motivational base, creative alternatives to intergroup violence can be considered.

Information, negotiations among leaders, and contacts between peoples can be utilized toward developing alternative courses of action. Then these, too, will become effective measures in reducing tensions. They become instrumentalities for developing the procedures for intergroup cooperation, instead of vehicles for intensifying conflict. As experiments show, groups pulling toward superordinate goals use information, negotiations among leaders, and interpersonal contacts in favorable directions. Over a period of time, these measures are conducive to changes in relationships between groups.

Intergroup systems within and among nations today have created spheres in which every group becomes increasingly dependent upon other groups. The predicament of one group is no longer merely its own concern, but also has impact upon others. The predicament of one becomes the predicament of all, small or large, weak or mighty. The condition of dependence of group upon group and nation upon nation is the necessary and sufficient condition for the recognition of superordinate goals shared with a sense of urgency.

To a world accustomed to thinking in terms of the privacy of group and national life, the realization that one group's affairs affect all is not immediate. For many potential superordinate goals to be recognized, the heavy hand of the past must be lifted. The superordinate goal must be singled out from the cumbersome complexity of accustomed practices that enmesh modern life. Ultimately, the successful pursuit of superordinate goals entails a soul-searching examination of the range of human identifications and human dependencies in actual living. It is a fact of human psychology that there is often a lag between the scope of humanity that we identify as "us" and the actual range of our dependence upon other groups whose actions affect our personal lives. In part, this lag is responsible for the large role played by the concepts of "luck" and "fate" in accounts of human experience. Being unaware of the actual range of humanity whose fortunes and misfortunes affect our own, we have no sensible explanation for many events. Thus, the incomprehensible is attributed to "bad luck" or to "man's fate." In the next chapter, we turn to an examination of the tasks suggested by this analysis.

9

Creative Alternative to the Predicament

In Retrospect

So far in this work, the main outline of a social psychology of intergroup relations has been presented. It started with a definition of the proper domain of the problem area (Chapter 1). In various connections, it was pointed out that not every case of friendship or dislike, cooperation or competition between two or more people falls within the domain of intergroup relations.

Only those states of friendship or hatred, harmony or conflict that stem from membership in groups fall within the domain, whether these involve collective action between groups or interpersonal relations between their individual members.

Membership in groups is not an idle affair. It establishes orientations and bounds for our transactions with other human beings, for good or for evil. It builds favorable or unfavorable images of ourselves and others which are more than momentary and situational. It defines aspirations, claims, and superiority-inferiority-equality arrangements between us and other groups that have unmistakable consequences on how we view and how we actually deal with the individuals in these other groups.

Group membership provides the person with favorable evaluations of "our way of life" and guideposts for appraising the way of life in other groups. It generates a sense of responsibility and loyalty to preserve and defend things that are *ours*. Maintaining and extending "our way of life" become cherished imperatives for all who are worthy and true, to the limit of the supreme sacrifice in times of crisis and external threat.

Demarcation of the problem area was followed by a discussion of the heavy hand of the past, with its accumulated myths and stereotypes, as it affects the urgent intergroup business of today (Chapter 2). It also guided us in evaluating psychological theories of aggression (Chapter 3).

People on the battleground cannot march against the barrage of deadly explosions just to satisfy whatever aggressive impulses they may have (innate or acquired). There is no orgy of catharsis for personal frustrations in braving such terror. Only fear of legal consequences, humiliation at the prospect of showing cowardice before comrades exposed to the same danger, or concern to give a good account of themselves to folks back home who count in their eyes (their reference groups) enable men to undergo such an ordeal. Only the well-balanced, sturdy, and steel-nerved can endure the ordeal. Therefore, technically developed nations institute elaborate screening devices to eliminate those who are unduly weak of nerve, trigger-happy, or impulsive.

Next, we discussed the orientation to intergroup relations that provides grounds for fruitful and testable hypotheses about conditions conducive to intergroup conflict and hostile attitudes, as well as conditions conducive to their reduction. On this basis, a program of research was initiated with design and techniques appropriate for testing the hypotheses (Chapters 4 and 5).

In the light of the findings and their subsequent verification by other investigators (Chapter 6), we evaluated relevant literature on certain dead ends in dealing with intergroup problems (Chapter 7), and studies on measures that can be effective when the necessary motive base has been prepared (Chapter 8).

Basic to all our work in social psychology has been our serious concern over validity, as aptly stated by Gerard Lemaine in reviewing one of our previous works on intergroup relations (Lemaine, 1964). We are convinced that social psychology, in concert with other social sciences, can contribute to the prediction and, eventually, constructive control of human relations. One prerequisite toward this end is the validity criterion in formulating problems and hypotheses, including the choice of study methods appropriate to them. Of course, this is not all. The real test for validity is the applicability of generalizations from research to the actualities of the larger scene.

Accordingly, we now turn to applying the formulations presented in this book to the vital problems of intergroup systems of the modern world. First, let us refresh our minds on the salient points in our analysis thus far.

FROM OUR PRESENT VANTAGE POINT

From the vantage point we have now reached, alternatives taken in intergroup relations can be seen more distinctly and in perspective. The dead ends reached from orientations that hypothesize self-generated, blind passions of the individual are there (Chapter 3). The vicious circle of assigning blame is there, as is the self-defeating formula of pitting power against power or deterrence (Chapter 7).

It is now discernible that conflict or harmony between human groups is not set in motion initially by the out-of-step stirrings of a few deranged individuals within their folds. Conflict or harmony starts from the courses human groups take as units. When a group takes a friendly or unfriendly course in its transactions with another group, the true and loyal members feel impelled to contribute their unique bit to the efforts needed for success. Failure or success of the course taken becomes very much a part of their *personal* experience.

Of course, groups are not static. Changes in groups are inevitable under changing circumstances. But change of a group's course comes about through the concerted action of those members who are most perceptive about their group's orientation and who have the foresight to see the alternatives ahead. Those who engage in Don Quixotic bravado seem to be shaken off in the process.

If we look closely enough, we easily find that the human group is not merely a collection of discrete individuals. Nor does it drop fully formed from nowhere. Every group, small or large, takes shape when its eventual members interact with mutual concerns.

Once it takes shape, a group cannot be undone by whim of the moment, even by the very persons who created it. Henceforth, its relations with other groups become primarily either clashes of interest between social units or of concerted or parallel actions as social units. The older alternative of each human group moving in a separate universe of its own has been obliterated through man's technological achievements which have made the fortress of distance between groups an undependable shield.

The tides of nationalism that have swept the world are becoming increasingly stronger. They tend to make nations overzealous in their pride and exclusiveness. But many observers of the contemporary scene have pointed out that any nation today regarding itself as self-contained is deluding itself, no matter how high its national pride. The dependence of nation upon nation is summarized in perhaps the best documented work on the rise and present state of nationalism (Shafer, 1955).

> Conversely, the nation-state and nationalism are possibly beginning to decline today because modern technology, the volume of industrial production and commerce, the speed of communication, and perhaps the enlightenment of many people are making national boundaries obsolete (p. 9).

Systematic experiments and surveys on friendly or hostile intergroup encounters in industrial, political, and community spheres point to the following propositions about intergroup relations:

Friendship and enmity between groups are group functions, not reducible to the ups and downs of interpersonal relations among individual members. A leading psychiatrist summarized the point as follows: ". . . it becomes increasingly clear that individual psychopathology cannot cast much light on the question of war . . . war is a group activity. Individuals fight but they do not wage war. This is reserved for organized groups" (Frank, 1964, p. 41).

The limiting condition in the rise of images and actions between two or more groups is the positive or negative nature of the functional relations between them. Two or more groups that transact with one another, directly or indirectly, will be competing with, disliking, and eventually fighting one another if winning a goal desired by one party amounts to loss for the other group(s). When victory thus means the humiliation or defeat of another group, vindictive attitudes arise, with the associated practice of casting blame on each other. Power will be pitted against power, with all of the meticulous planning, mobilization of resources, and preparedness executed by the more intelligent, sober, and highly trained within the fold. As Frank (1964) noted, "mentally healthy national leaders are as fully capable of leading a nation to war as unbalanced ones" (p. 41).

When a human group (rightly or wrongly) thus sees another group as an impediment to its course or as a threat to its existence or way of life, still other factors contribute to the developing conflict. The particular form of organization within each group, its practices and values in child-rearing, and the proportion of its members who are frustrated or well-adjusted individuals are *contributing* factors to the conflict, not its decisive cause. Ironically, the zeal with which members of a group pursue intergroup hostility will be proportional to the degree of solidarity and of cooperative interaction *within* the fold.

The sufficient condition for the rise of intergroup hostility gives us leads for finding effective measures for reducing hostility. If hostile attitude and deed are the outcome of groups confronting one another with incompatible and mutually exclusive claims, conversely, the reduction of hostility must depend on intergroup action to achieve goals that are desired by all parties and that require their cooperation. Friendly, fraternal attitudes develop when individuals in all groups feel that all will gain by pulling together toward superordinate goals.

WHAT IS CHARACTERISTICALLY HUMAN IN GROUP RELATIONSHIPS?

Now, without repeating the body of evidence, we can draw certain conclusions in regard to the workings of human nature in engagements between groups. Human nature has often been blamed for man's hostility and vindictiveness to man, and conscience has been credited with saving him from his destructive impulses. But we have seen that intergroup hostility arises from conflicts over vital interests and changes when the groups are directed toward superordinate goals. Apparently, both hatred and friendship are characteristically human, depending upon man's relationship to his groups and their position vis à vis others.

The characteristic and uniquely human process by which man becomes friendly or hostile to members of other groups is rooted in his nature and living with other men. The fundamental process is that men, living and acting with others, have always created bounds to regulate their attitudes and actions toward one another. These bounds define what is acceptable in attitude and action in dealing with others. They also define what is to be rejected as not permissible in interpersonal relations with others.

In other words, the fundamental human process is the formation of social norms. In interaction with others over a time span, man has always created yardsticks for appraising others and regulating his own feelings and actions in every sphere of living that is of lasting and significant import. Every human group, small or large, technically well developed or underdeveloped, on every continent has created such norms to regulate man's outlook, his feeling, his dealings with objects and people of lasting importance in the scheme of his day-to-day living.

The sphere of relations between group and group is no exception. Just as yardsticks arise for regulating behavior within groups, so relations between groups are invariably defined in terms of yard-sticks reflecting and codifying the positive or negative scheme of arrangements between groups. It is true that in many instances the norms men have created for treatment of outgroups have served to justify exploitation and domination. They have stabilized and codified superiority-inferiority practices.

The characteristically human process of forming norms to regu-late treatment of others may also result in the codification of friendly, fraternal attitudes and cooperative actions between groups. These too are characteristic of human beings. Always, norms at-tempting to justify and prolong human arrangements based on premises of one group that it is superior or has the right to exploit others have had multitudes of opponents. Acting in concert in their common humiliation, common inequities, and deprivation, human majorities have created their own formulations which have frequently triumphed as guideposts for ever-enlarging human formations. Thus, the *dignity of man, self-determination of peoples,* and *equality of opportunity* are among the norms that have been forged by men through the characteristically human process. They have become part of the conscience of many far-sighted people in various countries who are cautioning their fellow men against possible catastrophe, if the present drift of power pitted against power continues to its inevitable conclusion.

In the modern world, groups and nations have become dependent upon one another for their development, for their livelihood, and for their very existence. The main tide of men's struggles has been in the direction of more inclusive norms cutting across traditional rigid boundaries made obsolete by the increased dependence of people upon people in vital spheres of their existence.

The state of interdependence among nations and across con-tinents is creating yardsicks, practices, and agencies binding for all men in several spheres of life. Thus far, those most widely accepted and followed are found only in certain specific activities. The most overriding and common predicament of all nations — the question of human survival — is still crying for yardsticks and organizational structure that will be binding for all men.

The interdependence among people everywhere has increased at such an accelerated pace in this century that it collides with traditional rigid lines of sovereignty drawn by each group, as if it were still a self-contained island. The vision of superordinate goals compelling to all people is dimmed by those making a last ditch stand to conserve the myth that every group is a law unto itself, putting their own people at the peak of superior self-glorification and deprecating others as culprits and villains.

WHEN INTERNAL AFFAIRS OF NEIGHBORS BECOME EVERYBODY'S BUSINESS

Of course, a person's private feelings, private thoughts, and private preferences are his own. No one should meddle with them so long as they are truly private.

And of course, it should be the right and privilege of a family to run its own castle, to be the arbiter in conducting family chores, deciding what kind of meals it enjoys, what music it listens to, what books it puts on its shelves, what spending allowance is reasonable for the darling son or daughter. A family's preference should rule in altering or redecorating its house. If they so desire, members of a family have a perfect right to display furniture in the living room that is out of step with modern times and has outlived its usefulness. Those outmoded chairs and tables may be enshrined in happy memories, a part of the family's particular tradition.

But, should the family decide, for reasons of its own, to set the house on fire, at that moment the intention and deed cease to be private family affairs. They become the serious business of neighbors and the community. If it proves a nuisance or hazard for neighbors, even the private business of building a fire in one's own backyard becomes the business of the community.

There are city ordinances and state laws setting clear-cut limits as to what one can and cannot do, even in these and other relatively private spheres. The good people concerned with their own safety and the improvement of their community desire such rules and insist they be binding.

In brief, when a family engages within the privacy of its own house with its own resources and tools in activities that affect others, these actions do become the business of all. Therefore, communities lay down standards and rules, binding for all. Such standards, rules, and sanctions for offenders are not considered infringements on the sovereign dignity and will of the people in the community. The people can readily see that the limits placed upon what is acceptable and what is out-of-bounds are for their safety, well-being, and progress.

Yet, when people of a community view others not within their own set, the picture becomes complicated and fraught with problems. As members of their own circle, they become suspicious towards nonmembers. They use double standards, preferential to themselves. Their standards toward others reflect the vested interests of their own group. Their yardsticks for evaluating themselves and others are dictated by the interest and traditions of their closed circle. These yardsticks define personal identifications and loyalties that are at odds with the privacies of outsiders, hence foster strife with them.

Going much further, when we come to relations between nation and nation, we see each nation asserting a sovereign existence, the virtues of *its* ways of life, the righteousness of *its* course. Against such yardsticks, any adversary becomes offensive and wicked. The prospects of conciliation appear almost hopeless.

Is there a way out of the vicious circle, with each human group entrenching itself in a sovereign existence, unyielding in the absolutism of its yardsticks for evaluating its own stand and its own deed as well as for passing judgment on its adversary? At this crucial juncture, social psychology has something to offer that may prove to be its most substantive contribution.

The phrase "substantive contribution" is not used lightly. Its use does not imply that social psychology can hand down the specifics of blueprints, formulae of steps, or the instrumentalities involved. It is used, instead, to state that social psychology has grown sufficiently to provide pointers on the circumstances in which human beings move in concert with one another to establish rules for managing their relationships in an orderly and nonviolent way and for handling their differences. It can provide pointers on the conditions necessary for these rules to become personally binding.

Social psychology is still in the making. Its pointers can become more specific as it develops. As emphasized throughout this book, the social psychology which can make substantive contributions starts formulating problems on the basis of familiarity with the actualities of events, in this case with actualities in political, economic, industrial, racial, and national relationships within and between human groupings. Hypotheses for research are extracted from salient recurrences in these events, not from thin air. Methods and techniques for research are developed or chosen on the basis of whether they accommodate the essential features of the problem. Generalizations based on research and principles attained are not the terminal moment of truth. Their validity is checked and evaluated in terms of their predictive value for relevant events on the larger scene (Chapters 1, 4, 7, 8).

Guided by this conception of social psychology, we venture now to advance several propositions about the conditions in which human beings develop a code of conduct to regulate their dealings with one another and in which the rules of the code become binding in the consciences of the persons involved.

Interaction on the Level of In-Groups

When a number of individuals are motivated with compelling urgency towards common goals, they tend to engage in repeated interaction with one another. If, during interaction, the desired ends can be attained more advantageously through concerted activity, they invariably form, in time, an autonomous group of their own.

The main features of the group thus formed are an organizational pattern with unmistakable bounds and yardsticks (norms) for their activities toward the common ends. The "organization" (which need not be formally recognized) and the set of yardsticks (which need not be written rules) define their sense of "we-ness," cherished within the group and upheld by members in their dealings with outsiders.

In time, the standards shared in the "we" feeling become personally binding for individual members. The members who are worthy and true justify or condemn events within the *sphere related to their "we-ness"* in terms of their sense of identification with the group. Thus, the sense of solidarity, loyalty, personal accountability, and their "do's" and "don'ts" in *relevant* matters become part of the consciences of individual members.

These propositions are supported by a large body of research on human development and group formation, some of which is cited in this book. They are repeated here as basic for understanding the individual-group relationship and for discovering the sources of the constituents of the individual conscience.

Level of Interaction Between Groups That Are Subordinate Parts

By the phrase "subordinate parts," we mean group units that are parts of a larger formation, such as a community, a state or province, or a nation. As a rule, their functioning as units is regulated by a superordinate organization with authority at least in matters pertaining to their union. Examples are states or their counterparts within a federal union, or tribal units within newly arising nations.

The following propositions concern the rise of organizational forms and binding standards between subordinate units, such as those mentioned above:

When relatively small groups are prompted by common ends, exposed to common dangers, or otherwise recognize a common predicament, they tend to enter into transactions with one another. This tendency is promoted by proximity. It is also facilitated by advances in technology, for two reasons. Technology increases the ease of communication. Second, advances in technology ultimately increase the spheres of activity in which group becomes dependent on group.

Over time, the groups tend to band into a union in matters pertaining to their common predicament. This tendency varies according to the urgency of the predicament. The union thus formed is implemented in organizational forms and with rules of conduct that bear authority over the constituent subunits, in matters pertaining to their common predicament.

We emphasize the "common predicament" of groups as the salient condition for their banding together into a larger formation because a survey of literature on the rise of nation-states indicates that the sense of common predicament among constituents seems to be a more universal and potent factor than common culture, common language, or common religion. Of course, any or all of these contribute in varying degrees to the formation, depending upon circumstances (Emerson, 1960; Shafer, 1955).

At least in the case of new nations, the sense of common predicament is most typically a product of opposition to or rejection of a detested authority over them, a colonial power or a rival. Even in such cases, the common predicament does not develop full blown through spontaneous eruption. An enlarged sense of "we-ness" vis à vis a despised authority has to precede it. In the case of nation-states, this requires the development of political awareness toward self-assertion.

With the formation of a union, such as a nation-state, the sense of identity is proportionately enlarged. The authority for laying down rules, laws, and sanctions is transferred from the subunits to the federated organization or its agencies *in relevant spheres*. Over time, these yardsticks established by the larger organization come to define the individuals' loyalties, demarcate what is disloyal or treasonable, and become part of the individual conscience. The range of loyalties commanded by the subordinate unit and of loyalties commanded by the larger union varies over time with the scope of dependencies recognized between the various subunits.

THE WIDENING SCOPE OF INDIVIDUAL CONSCIENCE WITH INCREASED INTERGROUP DEPENDENCE

Common opposition to an enemy or oppressor can unify diverse and separate groupings, thus is conducive to forging a sense of identity among them in their joint plight. However, the common bonds quickly fade into memory when victory is achieved, unless there are other bases for dependence among the groups. The history of the American colonies, as well as current reports from new nations on revived regionalism, tribalism, or communalism, amply testify to this conclusion. The first sphere pre-empted by a union born in opposition to a common enemy is dealings with outside powers — foreign relations. Especially in other spheres, sharp divisions frequently occur over whose rules and standards are to be followed — those established by the union or those previously existing within particular groups composing the union.

At different periods, the histories of many nations reveal conflict and struggle between those upholding national standards of conduct and those loyal to the customs long established in smaller units. Incidents could be cited from the national development of Great Britain, France, Italy, and Germany as well as newer nations (Shafer, 1955). The psychological aspect of the problem is sometimes oversimplified as a simple conflict between personal identity as a Frenchman or Burgundian, a German or a Bavarian, an Italian or a Sicilian, an American or a Texan. The psychological problem is not this simple because personal identity is not simple. Personal identity may be tied to the larger union in specified spheres of life, while intimately linked with local tradition in others. When the union ventures to regulate conduct with standards that conflict with these cherished local customs, its efforts are resisted as violations to personal conscience. However, personal conscience does change as the spheres of interdependence increase among local groups constituting a union.

The case of the United States is particularly instructive in tracing the increased interdependence between the states and the subsequent development of yardsticks that supersede the sovereignty of the individual states. Dr. Maurice H. Merrill, Research Professor of Law at the University of Oklahoma, has summarized such developments for use in this volume, and elsewhere (1964) has analyzed the Civil Rights Act of 1964. We paraphrase and quote Dr. Merrill's illuminating account.

The union first achieved by the thirteen colonies after their common struggle against Britain, it will be recalled, was the loose Articles of Confederation between "free and independent states." In those times, writes Merrill, *when an American referred to his "country," he meant his state.* The several states treated one another very much like separate countries, levying tariffs, imposing embargoes, and sometimes disregarding the treaty obligations entered into by the union.

The formation of a new and stronger union was impelled by "realized interdependence" in certain important spheres: dealings with foreign powers and defense against the threat of war, commerce, and the promise of settlement in the vast westward lands. "Meanwhile, ties continued to be somewhat loose. Many people did not realize the change in legal theory brought about by the adoption of a Constitution that was to be the supreme law of the land. First one area and then another threatened secession when national policies seemed adverse to its interests. . . . Eventually, the concept of fundamental state sovereignty went down to defeat when the Civil War was fought to retain the South in the Union against its will."

The expansion westward and growth of commercial life after the Civil War gradually but irrevocably expanded the spheres in which federal laws were passed to command loyalty above strictly local and state concerns. The Interstate Commerce Act of 1887 initiated control over transportation rates and practices. It was successively extended to regulate the transport of "articles or persons," local laws or practices adversely affecting interstate commerce, state-owned enterprises engaged in interstate or foreign exchange, labor relations in plants supplied by and serving the international market (1937), and conditions of production (1941).

Merrill (1964) finds decisions under the Interstate Commerce Act (combined with the "sweeping clause" of the Constitution giving Congress power to "make all laws necessary and proper" for executing legislative and other government functions) ample precedent for the public accommodations provisions in the 1964 Civil Rights Act. Provisions for guaranteeing equal suffrage are otherwise supported by the 14th Amendment to the Constitution, which prevents any state from denying "equal protection of the laws."

The growth of federal union has gradually expanded in specific spheres of activity which became issues, especially as new conditions brought increased dependence of ways of life in one state upon those in the others. Rules emerging from early controversies over federal powers are now largely taken for granted. For example, the federal government's right to make treaties is undisputed by any state. In the recent dispute over the Mexico-United States border near El Paso, arising from the changed course of the Rio Grande, the citizens of the State of Texas had the greatest personal stake in the outcome. Yet, direct negotiations between Texas and the Mexican government would have brought indignant outcries up and down the country. Federal rules for dealing with foreign powers are so binding for the vast majority of citizens as to be personal conscience.

Since the Civil War, the superior command of the federal union for personal loyalty has also been binding in other matters. In LeRoy Collins' words, "most people have wanted a 'more perfect union' and less disjointed one, and have said so emphatically time and again — by ballot and by bayonet" (1964, p. 3). But this is not true in all spheres, as the recent civil rights struggles in both northern cities and southern states have shown. In this sphere, the conscience of many individuals has abided with the "sanctified institutions" of narrower circles of a "closed society," rather than the prescriptions of the constitutional union (Silver, 1964).

The genuine outrage of those resisting changes toward securing equal opportunity for Negro or other citizens reveals the extent to which the moral myths of discriminatory practices, rooted in local institutions, take precedence in this conscience and sense of loyalty. Loyalty to these myths, enhanced by the exhortations of power figures with political or other special interests in preserving "closed societies" or institutions, blind such individuals to the trends of life about them. Only the most alert in their midst dare to proclaim, as did a number of outstanding Southerners in the volume *We Dissent* (Norris, 1962), the "inevitable tide of equality and freedom which is moving humanity everywhere." Only the most sensitive can foresee their future, as did the Nobel prize-winning novelist and native of Oxford, Mississippi who wrote (Faulkner, 1956):

> We speak now against the day when our Southern people who will resist to the last these inevitable changes in social relations will, when they have been forced to accept what

they at one time might have accepted with dignity and good
will, will say, "Why didn't someone tell us this before? Tell
us this in time" (p. 12)?

Reciprocal Impact of Group on Group

The increased dependence of group upon group in the modern
world has broadened the scope of existing and incipient unions
among them. Above that, it has raised fundamental questions
about the notion of the sovereignty of social units or, conversely,
about when "private" affairs within groups become everybody's
business.

The problem was posed with reference to international problems
by Otto Klineberg in these words:

> There is a widespread view, incorporated in the Charter
> of the United Nations, that what happens inside the bound-
> aries of a particular nation is the concern of that nation alone,
> and is therefore not a legitimate field of action or even
> inquiry by the international community. This view is un-
> doubtedly justified for many internal phenomena, but at least
> in the special case of the relations between ethnic or "racial"
> groups, it cannot possibly be defended (1962, p. 174).

Here, we are concerned about the special contribution social
psychology could make to this problem. The propositions in this
chapter suggest an experimental approach to the general problem,
as previously proposed (Sherif and Sherif, 1965a). The basic
experimental variable can be conditions of the interaction between
individuals and between groups, as in the experiments reported in
Chapter 5. Through common goals requiring coordinated actions
and division of labor among individuals over a period of time, we
will again produce distinct, autonomous groups, say, a dozen of
them.

The autonomous groups will then be brought into contact, two
or three at a time. Their first encounters will be in situations that
embody compelling superordinate goals. We predict that the
groups will form a combination or union of some sort in those particular spheres related to their mutual dependence in attaining
these goals. In these spheres at least, procedures and rules will
emerge that will be binding for members of all groups in the
combination, thus enlarging their identification and code of ethics
beyond their in-group ethnocentrism.

The next problem is what will happen when these small combinations are brought together into functional relations with one another. Half of the combinations transact in situations embodying goals, whose attainment by one combination implies loss for others. The other half of the combinations will transact in situations embodying goals that are compatible.

We predict that those combinations who transact around mutually exclusive or conflicting goals will close their ranks within the combination. Conflict between combinations will follow, along with the rise of hostile attitudes and stereotypes, and the assertion of sovereign rights to proceed with the practices already established within each combination. For those whose initial contact centers around compatible goals, the establishment of still larger organizational units is predicted, to handle matters pertaining to common goals.

Finally, the sphere of dependence between the combinations is progressively broadened. A graduated series of dependence could be introduced, proceeding from highly specific contacts to increasingly central and pervasive issues.

When will the affairs within the conflicting combinations become a matter of such concern to others that they are no longer seen as internal affairs? How pervasive is the sphere of dependence between groups before they all take steps to establish binding rules that transcend those established by constituent combinations? We predict that concern over the internal affairs of other combinations and groups will increase as the scope of interdependence among groups increases. We predict an increased tendency to relegate intergroup conduct to a larger body as the sphere of common concern increases in scope, even though each organization maintains its autonomy and prerogatives in other respects.

Experiments that incorporate the major variables of group and intergroup relations enable us to specify the conditions that arouse intense emotions and the strategies they provoke. Of course, experimental simulation cannot claim to include more than essential properties of intergroup conflict and cooperation. At the very best, experimental simulation can be no more than a miniature paradigm. It is not possible to replicate the content of goals, the activities, or the length of time occupied.

Therefore, it would be naïve to presume that validation of predictions based on what happens in an experiment occupying a few weeks would be forthcoming in a few years in actual societal units such as nations. Groups do not give up their sovereign prerogatives easily, even in the spheres in which they are most interdependent with others for the survival and growth of their culture. Nations resist relegating the prerogative to wage war, even to an agency in which they are represented. It has taken destruction and suffering of great proportions to prompt nations merely to consider a superordinate agency with power to prevent the recurrence of destruction and suffering.

In a world lacking machinery and binding rules accepted by all groups to deal with concrete problems arising from their increased interdependence, the iron rule of in-group supremacy prevails. If a nation is powerful enough, it simply takes the law into its own hands when the internal affairs of another appear to impinge upon its interests. The self-righteous assumption that its interests are universal interests, thereby justifying the use of power and force, reflects ignorance of the causes of the problem. Because the causes are obscured, the consequences of the power play are inexplicable. It is not possible to understand why other nations react as they do, even if these reactions are confined to what is called "world opinion." In such states of actual ignorance or self-justified delusion about the causes and consequences, research findings may have value, despite the limitations mentioned above.

As members of groups ourselves, we invariably view questions about privacy and its invasion by outsiders in terms of our particular provincial loyalties. Our privacy is zealously protected. Our actions toward others are not seen as invasions, but warranted moves to protect our own private interests. Perhaps more than other endeavors, realistically conceived experiments might free us of such biases to explore the variables that affect our own group as well as others. The increasing interdependence among groups is one such variable, whose consequences need exploration.

LEVEL OF INTERACTION ACROSS NATIONS

The experiments outlined broadly above are not mere pipedreams. All that is proposed is exploration, in concrete miniature form, of the variables underlying trends already developing in the real world. The aim of the investigation may be better appreciated by examining some of these trends.

Interdependence of Nations in Specific Spheres of Living

Whenever nations become dependent on one another to the extent that a goal or practice in any sphere of life can be achieved only by cooperative effort, they tend to enter into transactions concerning the common problem. Coping with the problem effectively depends on their reaching binding rules for the benefit of all. In evolving such rules of conduct, each contributes actively.

When the nations have different practices in the sphere of common concern, the rules they evolve in their transactions cannot be confined within the framework of habitual practice of any single nation. To be effective, they must embrace the essential terms of all. To achieve rules that benefit all, each nation has to give up some part of its usual practice and prerogatives hitherto claimed as proper within the more narrow bounds of its sovereignty. This process has, in fact, occurred in numerous specific spheres of social life.

In a recent book on *International Law in a Changing World*, thirteen experts from different countries examined the trends toward evolving rules that cut across national boundaries and alter the closed-in conception of national sovereignty in particular spheres of life (Thirteen Experts, 1963). As one reads these contributions, one cannot help being impressed by the variety of specific activities for which international organizations have been founded because of the need for common yardsticks to be observed across national boundaries. For example, Professor Andre Gros of France observed:

> Let us first take another look at the international world and what it means. The world is by no means a simple thing; for, in addition to traditional sovereign States, it now includes many international organizations. . . . There are now, in fact, about one hundred such organizations. . . . Like the States, these organizations have now a recognized place in international law and within each of them the States' members negotiate with one another by what amounts to a new kind of diplomacy (p. 45).

From the contribution by Professor Roberto Ago of Italy, we may borrow a concrete sample of international organizations requiring a "new kind of diplomacy," which presumes yardsticks and rules appropriate to the cross-national problems:

> As early as 1875 the Universal Postal Union had been founded, in 1878 came a private international organization concerned with meteorology, in 1905 an international organization for agriculture, and in 1907 an international institute of public health. The fact remains, however, that the first really

large-scale international organization was the International La-
bour Office. . . . Other important steps taken at about the same
time were the creation of the Institute of Intellectual Cooperation, the Health Organization of the League of Nations,
the International Union of Telecommunications, and the Institute for the Unification of Private Law (p. 16).

C. Wilfred Jenks of the I.L.O. depicts the operation of the binding rules of conduct in the spheres of communication, transportation, and health, as exemplified in the experience of the individual:

> The invitation to deliver this lecture reached me by letter
> in Buenos Aires thanks to arrangements made by the Universal
> Postal Union. I cabled my acceptance through facilities oper-
> ated in accordance with the rules of the International Tele-
> communication Union. I later crossed three continents [to
> Geneva] by air services made possible by the rules and facil-
> ities of the International Civil Aviation Organization and the
> World Meteorological Organization. I was exempt from
> quarantine because I held a certificate of vaccination issued by
> the World Health Organization. Seven international organiza-
> tions had some part in my being here (p. 6).

There are common threads running through most of the contributions in this thought-provoking book. The trend is toward the
emergence of international organizations and norms for conduct in
various spheres of life, in the face of changing human arrangements. Despite this trend, law lags behind the developing interdependence of peoples in various spheres of life common to them
all, especially in the all-embracing domain of international disputes.
  The experiences of international agencies in more restricted
spheres of living show that the creation of effective organizations
across national boundaries requires norms for human conduct that
are binding for all concerned. Frequently, the evolution of these
common yardsticks requires change in the habitual practice of
particular nations in the matters of common concern. In these
spheres, the nations change their conception of sovereignty.
  The serious impediment to evolution of common and binding
norms for the resolution of international disputes is not inherent in
all transactions between nations. It lies in the adherence, especially
by the great powers, to premises and objectives dictated by the
confines of sovereignty which are at odds with the developing trend

of interdependence in human arrangements. A universal norm system and an effective organization for implementation should reflect the interests of people yearning for equality of all in the eyes of all. Achievement of such standards requires recognition of the common predicament faced by mankind today, pulling together across boundaries to deal with them, and ultimately common consent by nations to surrender that portion of their sovereignty that justifies aggressive war as a means of settling disputes.

Meanwhile, the expansion of cooperative efforts towards common objectives will aid the recognition of interdependence and establishment of procedures appropriate to it. These undertakings in specific areas, whether in science, commerce, learning, or agriculture, provide opportunities for working together toward a series of superordinate goals, which has proven effective in changing hostile attitudes. The beneficial effect of such a series of cooperative undertakings toward common objectives was noted by the president of the United States with the most powerful accumulation of technology to date:

> We are meeting with the Soviets to pool our knowledge about making fresh water from the oceans. These agreements by themselves have not ended tensions; they have not ended the risks of war. But because of them we have moved closer to peace (L. B. Johnson, 1964, p. 104).

The Trend Toward Widening
Self-Identity Revealed
by New Nations

A glance at the new nations is particularly illuminating in revealing the trends toward the interdependence of nations, probably in their most striking form. On the one hand, since World War II each of the more than sixty new nations has become sensitive in the matter of its sovereign self-identity, with all the pride in self-assertion that goes with it. On the other hand, these nations do make moves to be part and parcel of more embracing and even worldwide alignments.

It is not within the scope of this book to go into the particular forms of government or economic policies of the new nations. But it is highly pertinent to our topic to look at the self-images of new nations — eager to forge a stable identity, assertive, even cocky, yet ever seeking support and ties of a continent-wide and worldwide scope.

One way to account for the apparently contradictory trends is to look at the backgrounds of the leaders who guided these nations to independence and the problems they face in mobilizing the people toward development of their potentialities. Almost invariably, we find that the leaders of national independence movements have been men who had a modern education. Rupert Emerson (1960) documented the point with a long list of outstanding leaders of nationalist movements in Asia and Africa. Here is part of the list:

> Sun Yat-sen was a doctor who secured his lower education in Hawaii and his higher medical training in Hong Kong. Gandhi and Jinnah were British-educated lawyers, and Nehru was an Oxford man. In the Philippines Quezon and Osmena were both lawyers with extensive experience of the West. Luang Pradit in Thailand was a Paris-trained lawyer and Pibul Songgram studied military affairs in France. . . . If one turns to Africa the situation is the same. Habib Bourguiba of Tunisia is a Paris-trained lawyer, married to a French woman. Both Nnamdi Azikiwe of Nigeria and Kwame Nkrumah of Ghana studied at Lincoln University and elsewhere in the United States. . . . In Kenya, Jomo Kenyatta studied extensively in both London and Moscow, and Tom Mboya spent a year at Oxford; Julius Nyerere, head of the Tanganyika African National Union, is a product of Edinburgh University (pp. 197–198).

As is the case with leaders of nationalist movements, so the most active participants in the struggle toward a wider national unity have been those in closer contact with their Western rulers. "Thus in Kenya it was the Kikuyu, the instigators of the Mau Mau movement, who had the first and largest exposure to Western civilization, and other tribes, such as the Luo, have only slowly caught up with them" (Emerson, 1960, p. 358). The history of these differential contacts with Western civilization is documented in a book by Delf (1961). According to Wallerstein (1961), the roots of the Pan-African movement also extend from the West, especially the United States.

These facts are not surprising because the self-assertion of peoples through nationalism is a Western conception (Shafer, 1955; Emerson, 1960). As in Europe and America, nations arise from the wreckage of feudalism or imperialism. Proclaiming the self-identity of peoples in the same predicament within its bounds, nationalism thus rejects loyalties of more local scope, including tribalism and caste barriers.

Therefore, another irony arises: the nationalist leaders pursue a policy aimed at eventual liquidation of tribalism and caste, while the Western colonialists or neo-colonialists frequently follow a policy of encouraging local tradition and power (Legum, 1962, pp. 235–236; United Nations publication on Apartheid, 1963, p. 25).

Before independence, the ties uniting the people are forged in the common struggle against the colonial power or restraining authority. Thus the first manifestation of self-identity on a broader scope is based on their common rejection of an oppressor. Once independence is achieved, the common tie of opposition to outside authority is no longer sufficient to provide common bonds for national unity, especially in underdeveloped countries with strong and relatively unrelated circles having their own customs and traditions.

The strengthening of self-identity as a nation requires, in the modern world, recognition and acceptance by other nations. The new nations do seek such recognition. It is well established in psychology that recognition and acceptance by others are an integral aspect of building any kind of self-identity.

The new nations seek acceptance and support from those whom they feel have common problems. Thus, "although Africans identified themselves emotionally with their skin color, they were always intellectually willing and able to identify themselves with peoples of other colors who were in the same boat as themselves — the victims of white supremacy" (Legum, 1962, p. 41).

Once independence is achieved, the leaders turn zealously to mobilizing their people towards building industry, agriculture, an educational program, health programs, and other modern services (e.g., transportation, communication facilities). They face the Herculean task of telescoping time in changing unbelievably low standards of living, almost universal illiteracy, primitive agricultural practices, and the plagues of disease and early mortality.

Of course, the blessings of modern civilization and technology do not drop from the blue. Lacking the necessary capital, tools, and skills within their own boundaries, the new nations must depend upon outside support for their development projects, including support from the erstwhile colonial powers. Impatient to achieve the developments needed in the shortest possible time, the leaders develop forms of government and economic policies that they believe will promote the greatest speed and efficiency.

The dedication of efforts to building various development programs after independence is illustrated by one of the well-known leaders of a new nation: "With the achievement of Independence, the main theme of my speeches changed. I began to concentrate on the long-term objectives; economic freedom for Ghana and African emancipation and unity" (Nkrumah, 1961, p. 11).

Regardless of the particular form of government and economy, efforts toward planning are stressed. Planning contributes to the development and strengthening of a self-identity of national scope, in addition to specific purposes served. The political scientist Grundy (1964) stresses the twofold function of "centralized planning" with reference to Mali:

> First, and most obviously, it is a necessary instrument by which a country can shepherd its limited human and material resources in a more efficient way to achieve predetermined goals. Second, and perhaps more important to the politically conscious elite, *planning is a tool for national integration and unification* (p. 181, italics added).

For the latter purpose, several governments have initiated programs of "human investment" — voluntary labor in public and community projects. Aside from their utility in countries with limited funds and skilled labor, these projects serve to enhance the identification with the new nation:

> But the concrete results seem meager compared with the less tangible product — the building of a sense of national purpose and confidence among the masses. The projects mean a great deal to almost every participant. They serve to remind him that an economically backward people . . . can attain a higher standard of living (p. 189).

Embarked on projects for rapid development in industry and welfare that may appear too ambitious to some outsiders, the new nations necessarily are concerned about keeping a state of peace that will provide the needed time. The concern for peace is not peculiar to new nations of modern times. The same need for a period of peaceful development and nonentanglement with the disputes of great powers was experienced almost two hundred years ago, in what the sociologist Lipset aptly called *The First New Nation* (1963):

> The need to establish stable authority and a sense of identity led the leaders of the United States to resist efforts by "old states" to involve the young nation in their quarrels . . . (p. 90).

> The need to dissociate themselves from any deep identification with their former imperialist ruler, or with any major foreign power, is characteristic of all new states. All new nations must establish their own identities. . . . In the contemporary world, we have witnessed the rise of "neutralism" as the dominant tendency among the new nations of Asia and Africa. This concept of non-alignment has proved frustrating to the contenders in the Cold War who see the struggle as one between freedom and tyranny. They cannot see why nations which have just won their own independence can be so blind to an international struggle involving the issue of freedom. And the new nations' tactics of . . . playing the non-Communist bloc off against the Communist is regarded as a high-handed display of blatant self-interest (p. 62).

> Placing the issue in these terms ignores the fact that nations . . . act in terms of what they believe will enhance national growth and survival. The United States, in the early years of its independence, exhibited a similar equivocalness (p. 63).

The United States at the end of the eighteenth century was protected by a vast ocean, which made a policy of isolationism sensible, at least in principle. The present advance of technology has made child's play of distance and eliminated the feasibility of isolationism as a shield. The new nations know they are dependent upon more highly developed countries for capital, tools, and skills. They want to insure the time needed for realization of their development plans, even as they face constant pressures to line up with one or another great bloc. This pressure comes to peoples "still wary of imperial encroachment," in Emerson's phrase (1960, p. 392).

The upshot of these pressures and concerns is that the new nations seek security both in the United Nations and with other new nations in the same boat. In varying degrees and ways, all of them are internationalists. One significant direction of their internationalism is the banding together on a continental and cross-continental scope, as exemplified by the Pan-African and Pan-Asian alignments. The result is something new in human history: a widened scope of "we-ness" encompassing "Non-Aligned Nations."

> In addition to their membership in the United Nations, the Asian and African countries have demonstrated their internationalist inclinations in a number of meetings among themselves. Of these, the largest and most spectacular was the 1955 conference of twenty-nine states at Bandung, which repeatedly stressed the need for international cooperation in all spheres (Emerson, 1960, p. 393).

Since then, the alignment of non-aligned nations has widened. One recent declaration of this movement towards broadening of self-identity beyond national boundaries was the Cairo Conference of Non-Aligned Countries, in which "nearly half of the independent countries of the world have participated" (United Nations Reports, 1964).

These unprecedented events of recent history appear to reflect trends toward interdependence of nations, probably in exaggerated form. Nevertheless, the trend is so compelling that even the most powerful nations cannot control it. The new nations enter a world that tried its first organization in matters affecting international disputes less than a half-century ago, whose tragic demise was perhaps forecast when it was established as adjunct to the settlement of the first world-wide conflict of arms (U Thant, 1964). They enter the United Nations with no more eagerness and urgency than the great powers who founded it, but with perhaps a greater awareness of the contradictions between declarations of peaceful intent and power play in the cold war. A social psychologist cannot pretend to expertise on the technicalities of large organization. However, he can assess the evidence and agree that the organizational details of international bodies are less significant than whether or not the designs of their powerful members are compatible or incompatible with the purposes of the organization (cf. Etzioni, 1962).

AN IMPLICATION

From the material presented in the various chapters, there are implications for intergroup problems on the larger social scene.

As long as two or more groups within an intergroup system are in dispute and stick exclusively to their in-group premises in dealing with the adversary, tension, strategies for conflict, casting blame, and complacent self-righteousness on each side will continue. Prevailing morality and the dictates of individual conscience reflect the exclusive in-group position. Intergroup conflicts are never resolved so long as the conflicting parties appraise and orient their actions within the confines of their own interests and standards.

The basic condition for a larger sense of "we-ness," not torn by divided and contradictory loyalties, is the recognition of a common predicament leading to transactions to do something about it. The intergroup studies reported in Chapters 5 and 6, the cases of relatively tension-free-functioning of international agencies in specific spheres of life where various groups have a stake, and the banding together of nations all point to this effective base. These are the conditions for the rise of organizations cutting across group lines and the development of yardsticks binding and applicable to all. These are the prerequisites for the rise of effective morality, ultimately reflected in the conscience of individuals.

All successful solutions to intergroup problems involve a positive base: the cooperative activity of peoples gripped by realization of a common lot. The invariable product, over time, is a movement toward organization with binding rules of conduct in dealing with one another while doing something about the common problem. Such binding yardsticks for conduct arise in the spheres of life that have concerned them jointly. Always, time is required for them to become binding for all units or all peoples.

It should not be pretended that these things occur without affecting the in-groups in question. Intergroup process, for good or ill, does affect the groups involved. Only occasionally can the emerging organizational forms of an intergroup system be in the image of those prevailing within the respective groups. It follows that the rise of new, more inclusive standards and organizational forms requires the subordination of contradictory designs, practices, and standards prevailing within the groups *in spheres pertaining to their intergroup relationship*. Groups have always had and always will have private spheres of activity and interest that can be managed only by the parties directly involved, and that are, therefore, strictly "internal" matters.

One implication is that the notion of sovereignty of social units must be re-defined in matters that concern other groups or in which all have a vital stake. This conclusion was formulated by Fulbright in his scholarly book *Old Myths and New Realities:*

> In reality, the modern nation is the product of the historical evolution of human groups from their tribal beginnings to ever larger forms of social organization, not as the result of some mystical force of history, but in response to very *practicable* economic, military, and political needs. Until the twentieth century the building of nations represented a broadening of human bonds, but in the modern world of peoples made interdependent by scientific and technological revolution, the mythology of the absolute sovereign and self-sufficient nation delimits the bonds among men, confining them within political communities no longer capable of satisfying the requirements of security and economic growth. Indeed, the concept of national sovereignty has become in our time a principle of international anarchy (1964, pp. 86–87).

The broadening of human bonds is the prerequisite for morality in dealing with peoples outside the narrow in-group bounds, for creation of a widening sense of "we-ness," and for individual conscience in keeping with intergroup system free of tension and violence.

The trend is towards larger and larger dependence between peoples and toward the formation of organizations encompassing them. Historical evidence and empirical data of social science support this trend, even though they also show great human wear and tear, suffering, and reverses for intervals of time.

The great question is whether the trend toward interdependence will be permitted to culminate in the standards of conduct required from all, despite stubborn, last-ditch opposition by islands of resistance, or whether the trend will collapse in the worldwide holocaust of a thermonuclear showdown.

References

Ago, Roberto, 1963. The state and the international organization, in Thirteen Experts on International Law, in cooperation with the United Nations. *International Law in a Changing World* (New York: Oceana Library on the United Nations).

Allport, G. W., 1950. The role of expectancy, in H. Cantril, ed., *Tensions That Cause Wars* (Urbana: Univ. of Illinois Press).

Allport, G. W., 1954. *The Nature of Prejudice* (Reading, Mass.: Addison-Wesley).

Allport, G. W., and Postman, L., 1947. *The Psychology of Rumor* (New York: Holt).

Avigdor, Rozet, 1952. The development of stereotypes as a result of group interaction. Doctoral dissertation, New York University.

Barclay, C. N., 1963. A very real risk — war by accident. *New York Times Magazine.* May 5.

Benson, O., 1961. Simulation of international relations and diplomacy, in H. Borke, ed., *Computer Applications in the Behavioral Sciences* (Englewood Cliffs, N.J.: Prentice-Hall).

Berkowitz, L., 1962. *Aggression. A Social Psychological Analysis* (New York: McGraw-Hill).

Bethe, H. A., and Teller E., 1961. The future of nuclear tests. *Headline Series,* No. 145 (New York: Foreign Policy Assn., World Affairs Center).

Bierstedt, R., 1957. An analysis of social power, in L.A. Coser and B. Rosenberg, eds., *Sociological Theory* (New York: Macmillan).

Blake, R. R., and Dennis, W., 1943. The development of stereotypes concerning the Negro, *J. abnorm. soc. Psychol.,* 38, 525–531.

Blake, R. R., and Mouton, Jane, 1962. The intergroup dynamics of win-lose conflict and problem-solving collaboration in union-management relations, in M. Sherif, ed., *Intergroup Relations and Leadership* (New York: Wiley).

175

Blake, R. R., Shepard, H. A., and Mouton, 1964. *Managing Intergroup Conflict in Industry* (Houston, Texas: Gulf Publishing Co.).

Bogardus, E. S., 1928. *Immigration and Race Attitudes* (Boston: Heath).

Bogardus, E. S., 1947. Changes in racial distances, *Internat. J. Opin. & Attit. Res., 1,* 55–62.

Boulding, K. E., 1962. *Conflict and Defense* (New York: Harper).

Bronfenbrenner, U., 1961. The mirror image in Soviet-American relations. Cornell Univ. (mimeographed).

Campbell, D. T., and LeVine, R. T., 1961. A proposal for cooperative cross-cultural research on ethnocentrism, *J. of Conflict Resolution, 5,* 82–108.

Campbell, E. Q., and Pettigrew, T. F., 1959a. Racial and moral crisis: the role of the Little Rock ministers, *Amer. J. Sociol., 64,* 509–516.

Campbell, E. Q., and Pettigrew, T. F., 1959b. *Christians in Racial Crisis: A Study of Little Rock's Ministers* (Washington, D.C.: Public Affairs Press).

Cantril, H., ed., 1950. *Tensions That Cause Wars* (Urbana: Univ. of Illinois Press).

Cantril, H., and Buchanan, W., 1953. *How Nations See Each Other* (Urbana: Univ. of Illinois Press).

Clark, K. B., 1955. *Prejudice and Your Child* (Boston: Beacon Press).

Clemmer, D., 1940. *The Prison Community* (Boston: Christopher).

Collins, L., et al., 1964. *The Mazes of Modern Government: The States, the Legislature, the Bureaucracy, the Courts* (Fund for the Republic, Center for the Study of Democratic Institutions).

Delf, G., 1961. *Jomo Kenyatta: Towards Truth about the "Light of Kenya"* (Garden City, N.Y.: Doubleday).

Diab, L. N., 1963a. Factors affecting studies of national stereotypes, *J. soc. Psychol., 59,* 29–40.

Diab, L. N., 1963b. Factors determining group stereotypes, *J. soc. Psychol., 61,* 3–10.

Dollard, J., et al., 1939. *Frustration and Aggression* (New Haven: Yale Univ. Press).

Dubin, R., 1962. Leadership in union-management relations as an intergroup system, in M. Sherif, ed., *Intergroup Relations and Leadership* (New York: Wiley).

Emerson, R., 1960. *From Empire to Nation. The Rise of Self-Assertion in Asian and African Peoples* (Cambridge: Harvard Univ. Press).

Etzioni, A., 1962. *The Hard Way to Peace. A New Strategy* (New York: Collier).

Etzioni, A., 1963. A "peacemonger" answers some questions, *New York Times Magazine.* April 21.

Eysenck, H. J., 1950. War and aggressiveness; a survey of social attitude studies, in T. H. Pear, ed., *Psychological Factors of Peace and War* (New York: Philosophical Library).

Faulkner, W., *et al.,* 1956. *The Segregation Decisions* (Atlanta: Southern Regional Council).

Fowler, J. M., ed., 1960. *Fallout. A Study of Superbombs, Strontium 90, and Survival* (New York: Basic Books).

Frank, J. D., 1963. Conflict without war. Paper presented to Scientists on Survival. June 15.

Frank, J. D., 1964. Group psychology and the elimination of war, *Internat. J. Group Psychotherapy, 14,* 41–48.

Frazier, E. F., 1957. *The Negro in the United States* (New York: Macmillan).

Freud, S., 1922. *Group Psychology and the Analysis of the Ego* (London: Hogarth).

Freud, S., 1927. *The Ego and the Id* (London: Hogarth).

Freud, S., 1930. *Civilization and Its Discontents* (London: Hogarth).

Fulbright, J. W., 1964. *Old Myths and New Realities* (New York: Random House).

Gibb, C. A., 1954. Leadership, in G. Lindzey, ed., *Handbook of Social Psychology, Vol. 2* (Reading, Mass.: Addison-Wesley), 877–917.

Goldstein, Naomi, 1948. *The Roots of Prejudice Against the Negro in the United States* (Boston: Boston Univ. Press).

Goodman, Mary Ellen, 1952. *Race Awareness in Young Children* (Reading, Mass.: Addison-Wesley).

Gouldner, A., 1954. The problem of loyalty in groups under tension, *Social Problems, 2,* 82–88.

Gros, A., 1963. Peaceful settlement of internation disputes: mediation and conciliation, in Thirteen Experts on International Law, in cooperation with the United Nations. *International Law in a*

Changing World (New York: Oceana Library on the United Nations).

Group for the Advancement of Psychiatry, 1964. *Psychiatric Aspects of the Prevention of Nuclear War* (New York: 104 E. 25th St.).

Grundy, K. W., 1964. Mali: the prospects of "planned socialism," in W. H. Friedland and C. G. Rosberg, Jr., eds., *African Socialism*. Published for the Hoover Institution on War, Revolution, and Peace (Stanford: Stanford Univ. Press).

Hartley, E. L. (see Horowitz, E. L.), 1936. The development of attitudes toward Negroes, *Arch. Psychol.*, no. 194.

Hartley, E. L., 1946. *Problems in Prejudice* (New York: Kings Crown).

Hartley, E. L., and Hartley, Ruth E., 1952. *Fundamentals of Social Psychology* (New York: Knopf).

Hartley, E. L., Rosenbaum, M., and Schwartz, S., 1948. Children's use of ethnic frames of reference: an explanatory study of children's conceptualizations of multiple ethnic group membership, *J. Psychol.*, *26*, 367–386. Children's perceptions of ethnic group membership, *ibid.*, 387–398. Note on children's role perception, *ibid.*, 399–405.

Hartley, Ruth E. (see Horowitz, Ruth E.), 1939. Racial aspects of self-identification in nursery school children, *J. Psychol.*, *7*, 91–99.

Harvey, O. J., 1954. An experimental investigation of negative and positive relationships between small informal groups through judgmental indices. Doctoral dissertation, Univ. of Oklahoma.

Himmelweit, Hilda, 1950. Frustration and aggression: a review of recent experimental work, in T. H. Pear, ed., *Psychological Factors of Peace and War* (New York: Philosophical Library).

Hofstätter, P. R., 1957. *Gruppendynamik* (Hamburg: Rowohlt).

Holbrook, S. H., 1946. *A Century of American Ore and Steel* (New York: Macmillan).

Hood, W. R., and Sherif, M., 1955. An appraisal of personality-oriented approaches to prejudice, *Sociol. and soc. Res.*, *40*, 79–85.

Hovland, C. I., 1959. Reconciling conflicting results derived from experimental and survey studies of attitude change, *Amer. Psychologist*, *14*, 8–17.

Jahoda, G., 1961. *White Man* (London: Oxford Univ. Press).

Jamous, H., and Lemaine, G., 1962. Compétition entre groupes d'inégales ressources: Expérience dans un cadre naturel, premier travaux, *Psychologie Francaise*, 7, 216–222.

Jenks, C. W., 1963. Law, freedom and welfare in action for peace, in Thirteen Experts on International Law, in cooperation with the United Nations. *International Law in a Changing World* (New York: Oceana Library on the United Nations).

Johnson, G. B., 1964. Freedom, equality and segregation, in H. H. Humphrey, ed., *School Desegregation: Documents and Commentaries* (New York: Crowell).

Johnson, L. B., 1964. *My Hope for America* (New York: Random House).

Jones, L. W., 1965. The new world view of Negro youth, in M. Sherif and Carolyn W. Sherif, eds., *Problems of Youth: Transition to Adulthood in a Changing World* (Chicago: Aldine).

Jones, L. W., and Long, H. H., 1965. The negotiation of desegregation in ten Southern cities (Nashville: Race Relations Dept. of the American Missionary Assn., Fisk Univ. Mimeographed).

Katz, D., 1960. Current and needed psychological research in international relations. Paper to annual meeting, Amer. Psychological Assn.

Katz, D., and Braly, K., 1933. Racial stereotypes of one hundred college students, *J. abnorm. soc. Psychol.*, 25, 63–68.

Killian, L. M., 1962. Leadership in the desegregation crisis: an institutional analysis, in M. Sherif, ed., *Intergroup Relations and Leadership* (New York: Wiley).

Killian, L. M., and Grigg, C., 1964. *Racial Crisis in America* (Englewood Cliffs, N.J.: Prentice-Hall).

King, M. L., Jr., 1958. *Stride Toward Freedom* (New York: Harper & Row).

King, M. L., Jr., 1964. Letter from Birmingham jail, in B. Daniel, ed., *Black, White and Gray* (New York: Sheed and Ward).

Klapper, J. T., 1960. *The Effects of Mass Communication* (Glencoe: The Free Press).

Klineberg, O., 1950. *Tensions Affecting International Understanding* (New York: Soc. Sci. Res. Council Bull. 62).

Klineberg, O., 1962. Intergroup relations and international relations, in M. Sherif, ed., *Intergroup Relations and Leadership* New York: Wiley).

Klineberg, O., 1964. *Human Dimension in International Relations* (New York: Wiley).

Lapp, R. E., 1960. Nuclear war, in J. M. Fowler, ed., *Fallout. A Study of Superbombs, Strontium 90, and Survival* (New York: Basic Books).

Lawrence, P. R., *et al.*, 1961. *Organizational Behavior and Administration* (Homewood, Ill.: Dorsey and Irwin).

Lee, A. M., 1955. *Fraternities Without Brotherhood* (Boston: Beacon Press).

Lee, A. M., and Humphrey, N. D., 1943. *Race Riot* (New York: Dryden).

Legum, C., 1962. *Pan-Africanism* (New York: Praeger).

Lemaine, G., 1964. Book review of *Intergroup Relations and Leadership* in *Revue Francaise de Sociologie*, 2, 204–206.

Lewis, O., 1950. *Five Families: Mexican Case Studies in the Culture of Poverty* (New York: Basic Books).

Lippmann, W., 1922. *Public Opinion* (New York: Penguin Books).

Lipset, S. M., 1963. *The First New Nation: The United States in Historical and Comparative Perspective* (New York: Basic Books).

Long, Margaret, 1963. A Southern teen-ager speaks his mind, *New York Times Magazine*. November 10.

Luria, A. S., 1961. *The Role of Speech in the Regulation of Normal and Abnormal Behavior* (New York: Liveright).

Lynd, R., 1945. *Knowledge for What? The Place of Social Science in American Culture* (Princeton: Princeton Univ. Press).

MacCrone, I., 1937. *Race Attitudes in South Africa* (London: Oxford Univ. Press).

McDougall, W., 1923. *Outline of Social Psychology* (New York: Scribner).

McNamara, R. S., 1963. Testimony before House Armed Services Committee. Quoted by Senator G. McGovern, *Congressional Record*, August 2.

Manheim, H. L., 1960. Intergroup interaction as related to status and leadership differences between groups, *Sociometry*, 23, 415–427.

Meenes, M. A., 1943. A comparison of racial stereotypes of 1935 and 1942, *J. soc. Psychol.*, 17, 327–336.

Merrill, M. H., 1964. The constitution and civil rights. *Sooner Magazine* (Norman, Okla.: Univ. of Oklahoma Assn., March), 10–13.

Miller, N. E., 1941. The frustration-aggression hypothesis, *Psychol. Rev., 48,* 337–342.

Montgomery of Alamein, 1961. *The Path to Leadership* (New York: Putnam's).

Murphy, G., 1947. *Personality: A Biosocial Approach to Origins and Structure* (New York: Harper & Row).

Murphy, G., 1953. *In the Minds of Men* (New York: Basic Books).

Nehru, J., 1941. *Toward Freedom* (New York: John Day; Beacon paperback edition, 1958).

Nkrumah, K., 1961. *I Speak of Freedom* (New York: Praeger).

Norris, H., ed., 1962. *We Dissent* (New York: St. Martin's).

North, R. C., 1962. International conflict and integration: problems of research, in M. Sherif, ed., *Intergroup Relations and Leadership* (New York: Wiley).

North, R. C., *et al.,* 1963. *Crisis and crises.* Stanford Today. Series 1, No. 4, March.

Osgood, C. E., 1962. *An Alternative to War or Surrender* (Urbana: Univ. of Illinois Press).

Paul, J., and Laulicht, J., 1963. *In Your Opinion: Leaders' and Voters' Attitudes on Defense and Disarmament,* Vol. 1 (Clarkson, Ontario: Canadian Peace Research Institute).

Pear, T. H., 1950. Peace, war, and culture patterns, in T. H. Pear, ed., *Psychological Factors of Peace and War* (New York: Philosophical Library).

Pear, T. H., 1957. The psychological study of tensions and conflict, in *The Nature of Conflict.* International Sociological Assn. (Paris: UNESCO).

Perkins, Frances, 1946. *The Roosevelt I Knew* (New York: Viking).

Piaget, J., and Weil, M. A., 1951. Development in children of the idea of homeland and of relations with other countries, *Internat. soc. Sci. Bull.* 3, No. 3, 561–578.

Ram, Pars, 1955. *A UNESCO Study of Social Tensions in Aligarh* (Ahmedabad, India: New Order Book Co.).

Rappaport, A., 1960. *Fights, Games and Debates* (Ann Arbor: Univ. of Michigan Press).

Rappaport, A., 1964. *Strategy and Conscience* (New York: Harper & Row).

Razran, G., 1950. Ethnic dislikes and stereotypes: a laboratory study, *J. abnorm. soc. Psychol., 45,* 7–27.

Richardson, L. T., 1950. Statistics of deadly quarrels, in T. H. Pear, ed., *Psychological Factors of Peace and War* (New York: Philosophical Library).

Rokeach, M., 1960. *The Open and Closed Mind* (New York: Basic Books).

Rose, A., 1948. *The Negro in America* (A Condensation of an American Dilemma) (New York: Harper).

Russell, J. G., and Sherif, Carolyn W., 1966. Attitudes and reference groups of foreign students in the United States (in preparation). See also Russell, J. G., 1965. Effects of reference group identification on the relative importance ascribed to problems by Iranian and Latin American students at the University of Oklahoma. Doctoral dissertation, on file in the Library, Univ. of Oklahoma, Norman.

Sahlins, M. D., 1960. Origin of society, *Scientific American,* September.

Schneirla, T. C., 1946. Problems in the biopsychology of social organization, *J. abnorm. soc. Psychol., 41,* 385–402.

Schneirla, T. C., 1951. The "levels" concept in the study of social organization, in J. H. Rohrer and M. Sherif, eds., *Social Psychology at the Crossroads* (New York: Harper).

Schneirla, T. C., 1953. The concept of levels in the study of social phenomena, in M. Sherif and Carolyn W. Sherif, *Groups in Harmony and Tension* (New York: Harper).

Schneirla, T. C., 1964. Instinctive behavior, maturation-experience or development, in N. R. G. Maier and T. C. Schneirla, *Principles of Animal Psychology* (New York: Dover).

Scott, J. P., 1958. *Aggression* (Chicago: Univ. of Chicago Press).

Sears, R. R., 1960. The growth of conscience, in I. Iscoe and H. Stevenson, eds., *Personality Development in Children* (Austin: Univ. of Texas Press).

Secord, P. F., Bevan, W., and Katz, B., 1956. The Negro stereotype and perceptual accentuation, *J. abnorm. soc. Psychol., 53,* 78–83.

Shafer, B. C., 1955. *Nationalism: Myth and Reality* (New York: Harcourt, Brace).

Sheean, V., 1955. *Mahatma Gandhi: A Great Life in Brief* (New York: Knopf).

Sherif, Carolyn W., Sherif, M., and Nebergall, R. E., 1965. *Attitude and Attitude Change* (Philadelphia: Saunders).

Sherif, M., 1951. A preliminary experimental study of inter-group relations, in J. H. Rohrer and M. Sherif, eds., *Social Psychology at the Crossroads* (New York: Harper).

Sherif, M., 1954. Integrating field work and laboratory in small group research, *Amer. soc. Rev., 19,* 759–771.

Sherif, M., and Cantril, H., 1947. *The Psychology of Ego-Involvements* (New York: Wiley).

Sherif, M., Harvey, O. J., White, B. J., Hood, W. R., and Sherif, Carolyn W., 1961. *Intergroup Conflict and Cooperation. The Robbers Cave Experiment* (Norman, Okla.: Univ. of Oklahoma Book Exchange).

Sherif, M., and Hovland, C. I., 1961. *Social Judgment* (New Haven: Yale Univ. Press).

Sherif, M., and Koslin, B., 1960. The "institutional" vs. "behavioral" controversy in social science with special reference to political science. Norman, Okla.: Institute of Group Relations.

Sherif, M., and Sherif, Carolyn W., 1953. *Groups in Harmony and Tension* (New York: Harper).

Sherif, M., and Sherif, Carolyn W., 1956. *An Outline of Social Psychology,* rev. ed. (New York: Harper & Row).

Sherif, M., and Sherif, Carolyn W., 1964. *Reference Groups: Exploration into Conformity and Deviation of Adolescents* (New York: Harper & Row).

Sherif, M., and Sherif, Carolyn W., 1965a. Research on intergroup relations, in O. Klineberg and R. Christie, eds., *Perspectives in Social Psychology* (New York: Holt, Rinehart and Winston).

Sherif, M., and Sherif, Carolyn W., eds., 1965b. *Problems of Youth: Transition to Adulthood in a Changing World* (Chicago: Aldine).

Sherif, M., White, B. J., and Harvey, O. J., 1955. Status in experimentally produced groups, *Amer. J. Sociol., 60,* 370–379.

Silver, J. W., 1964. *Mississippi: The Closed Society* (New York: Harcourt, Brace and World).

Sinha, D., 1961. Caste dynamics: a psychological analysis, *Eastern Anthropologist, 13,* 159–171.

Smith, Lillian, 1964. The mob and the ghost, in B. Daniel, ed., *Black, White and Gray* (New York: Sneed and Ward).

Stevens, F. B., 1960. White man's future in Black Africa, *U.S. News and World Report*. August 22, 60–66.

Stogdill, R. M., 1948. Personal factors associated with leadership, *J. Psychol.*, 25, 35–71.

Stogdill, R. M., 1959. *Individual Behavior and Group Achievement* (New York: Oxford Univ. Press).

Stouffer, S., *et al.*, 1949. *Studies in Social Psychology in World War II. Vol. 2, The American Soldier* (Princeton: Princeton Univ. Press).

Sussman, M. B., and Weil, W. B., 1960. An experimental study on the effects of group interaction upon the behavior of diabetic children, *Internat. J. soc. Psychiatry*, 6, 120–125.

Tajfel, H., and Wilkes, A. L., 1963. Salience of attitudes and commitment to extreme judgments in the perception of people, *Brit. J. soc. clin. Psychol.*, 2, 40–49.

Teller, E., 1961. See Bethe and Teller.

Thirteen Experts on International Law, in cooperation with the United Nations, 1963. *International Law in a Changing World* (New York: Oceana Library on the United Nations).

Time, 1965. January 22, 14–18.

Time, 1963. May 24, 39.

Tolman, E. C., 1942. *Drives Toward War* (New York: Appleton Century).

Tumin, M. M., 1963. Race and intelligence, in H. H. Humphrey, ed., *School Desegregation: Documents and Commentaries* (New York: Crowell).

U Thant, 1964. The League of Nations and the United Nations. Text of address at the University of California: (New York: United Nations).

United Nations, 1963. *Apartheid* (New York: United Nations Office of Public Information).

United Nations Report, 1964. Report addressed to the Secretary General, October 29. General distribution (mimeographed).

Wallerstein, I., 1961. *Africa: The Politics of Independence* (New York: Vintage Books).

Warren, R. P., 1956. *Segregation: The Inner Conflict in the South* (New York: Random House).

Wertheim, W. F., 1956. *Indonesian Society in Transition, A Study of Social Change* (The Hague: W. von Hoeue).

White, L. A., 1959. *The Evolution of Culture* (New York: McGraw-Hill).

White, R. K., 1961. Misconceptions in Soviet and American images. Amer. Psychological Assn. Convention, New York, September.

Whyte, W. F., ed., 1955. *Money and Motivation* (New York: Harper & Row).

Williams, R. M., Jr., 1964. *Strangers Next Door* (Englewood Cliffs, N.J.: Prentice-Hall).

Zaidi, S. M., and Ahmed, M., 1958. National stereotypes of university students in East Pakistan, *J. soc. Psychol.*, 47, 387–395.

Name Index

Subject Index

189